SEW SERENDIPITY *Bags*

Fresh + Pretty Projects to Sew and Love

KAY WHITT

SEW SERENDIPITY *Bags*

Fresh + Pretty Projects to Sew and Love

KAY WHITT

KRAUSE PUBLICATIONS
CINCINNATI, OHIO

INTRODUCTION

Having a collection of versatile bags is such an essential part of every woman's wardrobe. We use bags in so many ways and for so many different functions. No matter how many bags we have, we always yearn for more! In this book, I have put together a collection of twelve distinct designs that expand into 20 projects for bags that will multitask quite nicely for just about anyone.

Each bag has its own individual style from sophisticated to cool and casual, while keeping function and ease of use at the core of each design. I want you to feel that what I have offered to you here is merely a stepping-stone to take each of these designs and make them your own. We all have a unique vision for what is the "ultimate" in a bag. My goal is for you to feel confident with adding or subtracting details to make each bag the "ultimate" for you or whomever you might be making the bag for.

I love to design and make bags! The challenge of making a bag to suit a certain need is what I find the most intriguing about the process. I usually start with pencil and paper and make a simple sketch of the design I have in mind. I then think about the finished dimensions of the bag and assign measurements to the different components of height, width and depth. Then comes the fun part: adding seam allowances, shaping the pieces and figuring out the best way to put the parts together that makes sound construction sense, as well as addressing the overall durability of the design. This is obviously the most time-consuming portion of the work and where prototypes come to life in my process. Throughout the book, you will see a sketch of where my design started and then the actual photographs of the finished project. In a lot of respects, the design will hold true to the original sketch, but sometimes a detail here or there will change based on what happens during the prototype phase. I like to let the design tell me where to go next. My hope is that by seeing into my process a bit, you can apply your own creativity here and there.

Indispensable Notions

MEASURING TOOLS

Dressmaker's Measuring Tape: This tape is about 60" long and is very flexible. It's perfect for taking body measurements and other varied measuring uses when you need a flexible tool.

Quilting Ruler: I love my 24" × 6" quilting ruler! It is transparent so I can use it for a variety of measuring needs. I use it often for cutting strips of fabric with my mat and rotary cutter. Even if you don't quilt, this is a great tool.

MARKING TOOLS

Marking Pencils: There is a variety of tools out there, from chalk pencils to air-soluble markers. I've recently discovered Sewline marking pencils. What can I say about these pencils? They're the best! They work like a mechanical pencil with a retractable lead and even come with a handy eraser that really does remove the marks from the fabric. They come in a variety of colors. I have tried many marking pencils over the years, and these are, hands-down, the best. These can be purchased at your local quilt shop or online.

IRONS & IRONING BOARDS

Irons: I have a Rowenta Steam Generator. If you do a lot of ironing, you need this tool. It has fantastic steam power, which makes ironing so easy! It holds four cups of water in the tank, which is about 1½ solid hours of steam. This means you can pretty much sew all day and not run out of steam. How is that for awesome?

Ironing Board: I have a Rowenta Professional Ironing Board—I love this little beauty! It features an extra-wide board, making it a great location to lay out pieces to get them ready for ironing. It also has a shelf to the side for holding the iron and a lower shelf for holding other items. It's heavy duty and well balanced so that it does not tip easily.

Pressing Cloth: I use a plain white tea towel as a pressing cloth. A pressing cloth is invaluable when working with heat-sensitive materials, such as laminated or napped fabrics (like velvet or velveteen).

CUTTING TOOLS

Scissors: I have three pairs of 6" Gingher scissors. I keep them stashed at different locations in my studio so that a pair is always handy. These are tough scissors that retain their sharpness for a long time and can cut through many layers of fabric at once. They have great points, which help to clip curves and snip into seam allowances where needed.

Thread Snips: I love having a pair of thread snips by the machine to clip threads. They fit easily into your hand and are ergonomically friendly.

Rotary Cutter and Mat: I use my rotary cutter and mat all the time. These tools, along with a quilting ruler, really are the best way to cut accurate squares, rectangles and strips.

Seam Ripper: It is inevitable that you will need a seam ripper from time to time to do some "un-sewing." Not fun, but sometimes necessary. I also like to use these for opening buttonholes; be careful if you do—these are very sharp and can cut beyond the end of the buttonhole!

OTHER TOOLS

Point Turner: I use a bamboo skewer or an acrylic point turner to fully turn out pieces. Because both of these have a duller point than scissors, you're less likely to punch through a corner. I keep two or three acrylic point turners on hand in the studio at all times.

Pins: I use a variety of different-sized safety pins to turn tubes of fabric right side out. A lot of people like to use different turning tools, but I prefer the good old safety pin for this task. And I always have a supply of dressmaker's pins on hand. I like the ones with the pearlized heads—they are extra-long and very sharp.

Pattern Tracing Cloth: I use a nylon product that is translucent with a grid of dots spaced 1" apart. It's virtually impossible to tear, making it superior to using tissue scraps for tracing pattern pieces. You can write on it with pencil or pen and it can be gently pressed with low heat. It comes pre-packaged in 5-yard lengths or can be purchased by the yard and it is 36" wide.

Needle-Nose Pliers: This tool is perfect for bending the prongs of latches and snaps. I've also used them to pull out bits of broken machine needles. (Yes, it occasionally

happens!) These are easily found at just about any hardware or craft store at an inexpensive price. I prefer the small size; they fit well in my hand and are big enough for the job.

Grommet Pliers: These are wonderful for installing grommets. The ⅜" size seems to be common and is the one I used for the projects in the book. This tool usually comes with a few grommets to get you started.

Awl: An awl is a very pointed tool, much like an ice pick. I like to use it for starting a hole, like for the eyelets used on the Laptop Messenger Bag and Convertible Backpack.

Your Machine and Specialty Presser Feet

Perhaps the most important tool of all is your sewing machine. Get the best one you can afford. Even if you have to forego the bells and whistles, get a basic machine from a reputable company.

There are also several specialty feet you may want to invest in that are referenced throughout this book.

Open-Toe Embroidery Foot: Believe it or not, this is the foot that I do *all* of my sewing with. That's because it lets me see where the needle is at all times.

Denim Foot: This foot is ideal for sewing through many layers of fabric and stabilizer. It gives additional support to the needle and thus you have less needle breakage.

Teflon-Coated Foot: This foot is great for sewing with laminated cottons. It enables the fabric to flow easily under the machine foot instead of getting caught up, as with a regular foot.

Zipper Foot: This foot is indispensable for adding zippers to bags.

Ruffler Attachment: It's a bit expensive, but if you love ruffles, it's worth it. It gives you perfect ruffles every time.

Walking Foot: This foot enables you to feed multiple layers under the needle evenly, particularly when batting or fleece is sandwiched in between. If you're quilting your own fabric for the Tulip Tote or Quilted Duffel, this is a great addition to your sewing arsenal. The walking foot is also a good alternative to the Teflon-coated foot when sewing laminated cottons.

Bag Hardware

Hardware is like the icing on the cake for a bag. If the icing is poorly chosen or made (or bought—*gasp!*), the end result is affected. Having said that, it is hard to find good hardware—maybe that's why it is called that! I have searched high and low, so I have done a lot of the grunt work for you. Below is a detailed list of my preferred hardware elements and why I think they make a difference. For the harder-to-find items, check out the Resources section of the book.

Zippers: Zippers scare a lot of people. If you merely mention installing one, some people's eyes will widen with horror! Most of the time, a zipper is an easy installation. In the marketplace, there are a lot of zippers to choose from. The question is, which one do you use? Well, that can vary, but my preference for the exterior closure of a bag is the sport zipper (1). These are the chunkier-type zippers that you see in jackets and heavier bags. They can be made from vinyl or metal. I prefer the vinyl ones because I can color-coordinate them with the fabrics and the teeth aren't as sharp (helps prevent damage to the items you're carrying, or even scratching yourself as you reach in and out of the bag). Sometimes a supply list will call for a separating zipper (1), usually due to a construction step that cannot be completed with a closed-bottom zipper. If one is called for, *do not* make a substitution! If a separating zipper is not specifically required, then you can use either type. It's simple to make a separating zipper into a closed one, and I tell you in the instructions where needed. For the interior of a bag, like a zippered pouch or pocket, I list a lighter-weight closed-bottom zipper (2) (commonly used in garment-making) since the added bulk of a sport zipper isn't needed in this application.

Zipper Charms: I *love* zipper charms (3). You might know them better as zipper pulls. Of course, these are just a little extra accessory to pretty up the bag, but they do serve a functional purpose as well. Not all zippers are created equal when it comes to the built-in zipper pull; some are small and hard to get hold of. Zipper charms just make a bag easier to open and close.

D-rings, Double Loop Sliders and Swivel Clasps: I use these throughout the different projects. D-rings (4) are a great way to add a shiny touch to a bag handle where it attaches to a bag. In some instances, these are added for function, such as for the Convertible Backpack. I like a nice heavy D-ring without a physical join. In my opinion, these have more presence and make the bag more professionally finished. The double loop sliders (5) are a nice touch when a bag needs an adjustable-length handle. These are wonderful because you can decide whether to wear your bag across the body or over the shoulder. Lastly, the swivel clasp (6) is wonderful for adding versatility to a handle, such as for the Cross-Body Purses. Because this clasp has the ability to twist, the handle can remain flat against the body during wear, making the bag more comfortable and attractive.

Buckles: Buckles (7) are great for adding a nice touch to the handle, such as for the Ruffle Hobo Bag. This bag's handle is actually in two parts, so it has to be joined by overlapping and sewing the finished pieces, or adding a fun buckle. I obviously prefer the fun buckle! These come in a variety of finishes and shapes.

Magnetic Snaps: Magnetic snaps (8) are probably the most common type of closure for a sewn bag. They are easy to find and easy to install. Over time, these can cause the fabric to tear, so I like to reinforce the wrong side of the fabric with a small piece of interfacing or Peltex before installation so that the fabric can withstand the repeated use of the snap.

Latches: Latches (9) can also be called twist locks, depending on the manufacturer. I like this type of hardware as it brings another shiny little detail to the exterior of the bag. Most of these latches have a prong installment, so they are similar to installing a magnetic snap in most cases. There are a few exceptions. I have run across a type that actually has a front and back piece that screw together. These are nice also and are simple enough to install.

Hook and Loop Tape: This is a great way to add an invisible closure to a pocket flap. I use hook and loop tape (10) throughout the book on the exterior pocket flaps. Commonly referred to as Velcro, it is easy to find and install. When you purchase it, be sure that you are buying the "sew-in" type and not the stuff with adhesive. The adhesive can do seriously wicked things to the internal workings of your sewing machine!

Buttons & Brooches: Never underestimate the power of a good button or brooch! I always have my eye out for ones with good "bling" power. Buttons are one of my personal favorites because they are easily accessible and simple to install. They make such a nice statement on the Foldable Shoppers as well as on one of the Socialite Handbags. They are great on their own as a statement or to complete the center of a wonderful fabric flower. I also love a good pin! I love vintage brooches, but I've found some great ones in discount stores and in craft shops. Check out the Tulip Tote to see how a brooch can add that perfect finish. I even added just a touch of tulle to the back of the pin before attaching it to the bag. And you can't miss the fabulous silk flower on the Laptop Messenger— that one's a show-stopper! You can also make your own little embellishments. Check out the fabric flowers on the Multi-Tasker bags. Those are easy and fun to make; I have a special tutorial under "Summer Flower" on my blog.

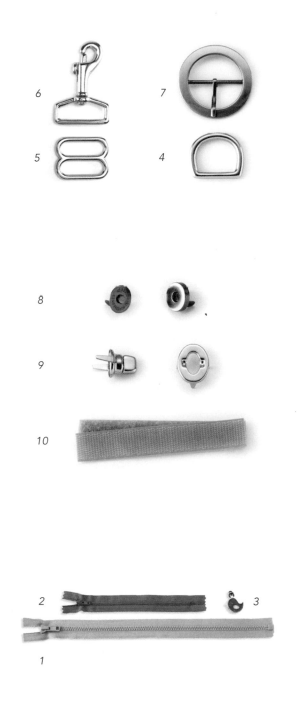

Using a Ruffler Attachment

The ruffler attachment allows you to make uniform gathers or pleats with the sewing machine rather than pulling threads by hand.

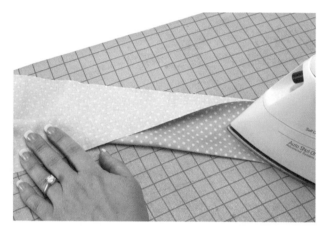

1 Most of the ruffles for the projects are created from a strip that has been folded in half lengthwise, wrong sides together, and pressed.

2 Place the strip between the blades on the ruffler attachment. Using a straight stitch, sew about ¼"–⅜" from the raw edges. The project will detail whether to set the attachment to gather at every stitch or every sixth stitch.

3 Adjust the ruffles by hand, if needed, smoothing them out to make them easy to work with.

4 Press the ruffles flat to create a more pleated appearance.

Making Gathers

Ruffles and gathers are a great way to add fullness to a pattern, adding a sweet flirty twist. Check out how cute they can be on the Socialite Handbag (page 90).

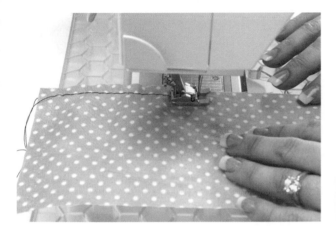

1 Using a long, straight stitch, sew about ¼" away from the raw edge.

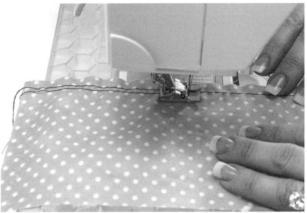

2 Sew another line of long, straight stitches about ⅜" away from the edge.

3 Wind the bobbin threads around your fingers and gently pull the threads to create gathers in the fabric. Keep pulling and positioning the gathers along the length of the fabric until you achieve the fullness you want.

Cutting on the Bias

Cutting strips on the bias helps you to easily bind the edges of a curved piece (such as the flap of a bag). This is because fabric cut on a 45-degree angle has a bit of stretch.

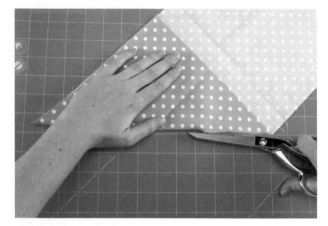

1 To cut on the bias, begin by folding up a corner on the diagonal and trimming it off.

2 Fold the fabric along this newly cut edge.

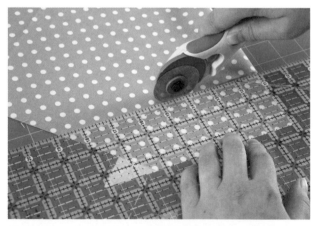

3 Using a rotary cutter, cut the strips to a specified width according to your project instructions. Cut however many strips it will take to go around the piece you are binding.

4 Place the ends of the strips together at a 90-degree angle. Piece the strips right sides together along the angled edges with a ¼" seam allowance.

5 Trim off the points.

6 Press the seams open.

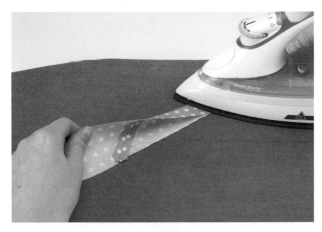

7 Fold the strip in half lengthwise with wrong sides together and press.

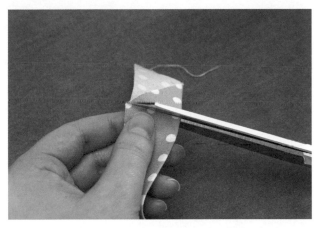

8 Trim the angled seam edges to straighten.

9 Open out the strip once more. Fold the narrow edge back ½" to the wrong side and press.

10 Fold the strip in half lengthwise with wrong sides together once more and press briefly. Add the bias strip as directed in the project instructions.

Making Handles

Many of the handles for the projects are made in the same manner. Be sure to piece the strips together as instructed per project to ensure the proper length as well as width. Once the strips have been cut, pieced and interfaced on the wrong side of fabric, follow the steps below to create the handles.

1 Place two strips right sides together and stitch down one of the long sides with a ½" seam allowance. Press the seam open.

2 Fold in one of the outer raw edges so that it just touches the raw edge of the seam allowance and press.

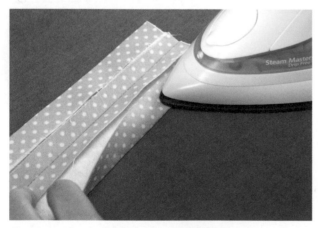

3 Repeat for the other outer raw edge.

4 Fold the handle strip in half along the seam, with wrong sides together, and press.

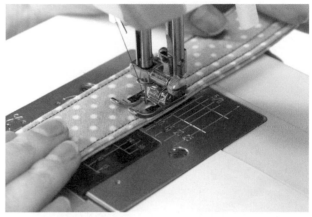

5 Edgestitch down the long open side of the handle, then down the long finished edge. To edgestitch, begin at one end and follow the finished edge all the way around a piece. I like to stay within 1/16" to 1/8" away from the edge for this stitching.

6 Topstitch each side. To topstitch, begin again at the same end where the edgestitching started, only this time, complete the stitching approximately 1/4" in from the previous stitching line. Notice how I use the outer edge of my machine foot to gauge the distance evenly all the way around the piece.

Repeat for any remaining handle strips, then trim the handles down to the length specified in the instructions.

Pivoting

When edgestitching or topstitching handles, I like to pivot the piece and stitch across the end. Pivoting at the end of the handle saves time and means that there will be fewer threads to trim later.

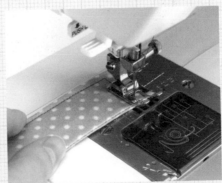

1 When you are within 1/8" of the edge, stop with the needle firmly in the fabric. Lift the presser foot, and rotate the fabric.

2 Drop the presser foot, and continue sewing.

Installing a Double Loop Slider

Installation of a double loop slider enables the handle to be adjustable. This is particularly handy on the Cross-Body and Convertible Backpack projects. This is a simple installation once you know how to do it.

1 Feed the handle end through the slider.

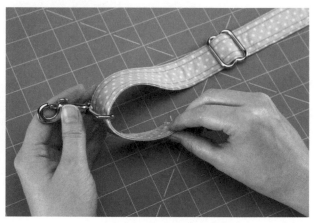

2 Put the end of the handle through the D-ring or swivel clasp, whichever applies to the project.

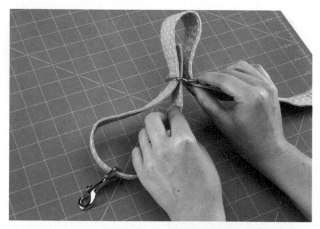

3 Pull up some slack in the handle portion that feeds through the slider. Slip the end of this handle under the slack, and next to the middle bar of the slider.

4 Feed the end over the middle bar, keeping it under the slack.

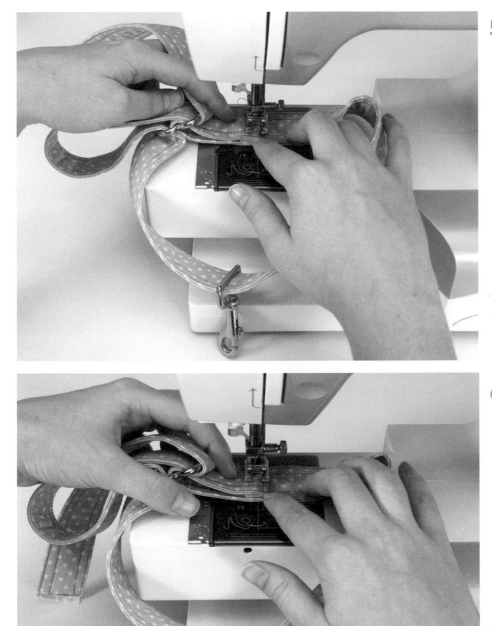

5 Fold over the end of the handle ½" and place that end as close as possible to the slider while still being able to machine-stitch to secure it.

6 Stitch across the handle end. Repeat for added durability.

Installing Grommets

Grommets (or eyelets) allow for a finished-edge hole to be put into a bag. These are used for the media pockets on the Laptop Messenger, Convertible Backpack and Multi-Tasker Bag.

1 To install a grommet, place the front portion onto the piece, following the placement in the project instructions. Use a temporary marking pencil to trace the inside of the circle.

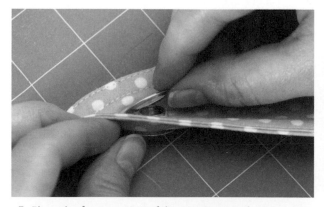

2 Start the opening with an awl.

3 Enlarge the opening with a sharp pair of scissors.

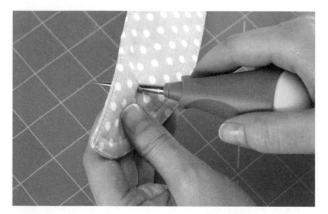

4 Place the front portion of the grommet in the opening with the back portion on the other side of the piece.

5 Use grommet pliers to attach the pieces around each other and secure to both sides of the fabric.

Trimming and Clipping

When you're working with multiple layers of fabric *and* stabilizers, the bulk can really build up at the seams. Trimming the seams down and clipping them along curves enables the finished seam to lay flatter and reduces bulk, producing a nicer finish. When trimming close to the stitches, be careful! Cutting stitches will create an ugly opening in your seam.

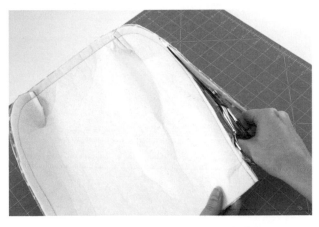

1 Use sharp scissors and begin at one end of the seam.

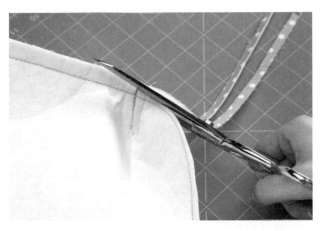

2 Trim close to the stitching and follow the seam all the way to the other end. Once the trimming is complete, check to make sure that stitches are still intact. Sew again over any cut stitches.

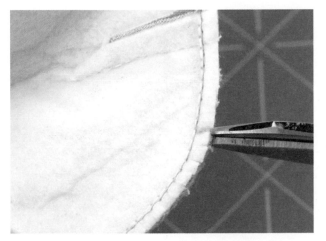

3 If the shape of the bag has curves along the sides, clip those by completing a series of snips through all thicknesses of the remaining seam allowance, about ¼" apart, being careful that you don't clip through the stitches.

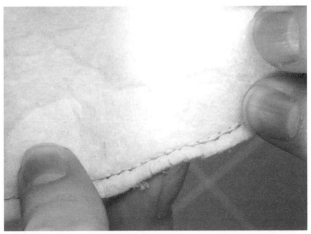

4 Check the stitching once more after clipping is completed to be sure that none were clipped. Sew again over any clipped stitches.

Pressing Techniques

When working with stabilizers, sometimes you will get a crinkly effect once a bag is turned right-side out. Not to worry! The iron can take care of that. But even more handy, the iron can help shape the bag. Stabilizers respond to heat and steam, softening to let you shape them. You'll want to steam and press the bag at multiple stages—usually before you add the lining, once the lining has been added and again at the end of the construction process. Repeat this process until the bag has a smooth, professional appearance.

1 To get a professional finish, begin with the bag sewn together and right-side out. Wad up a tea towel in your non-dominant hand and hold it inside the bag wherever the bag needs to be smoothed. Use the tea towel to shape the bag and also to protect your skin from the heat and steam.

2 If the bag has curved corners (like here) or rounded sides, wadding up the tea towel and stuffing it into the curve allows you to press and shape without flattening.

3 For sharp creases (often found along seams and corners), determine where you want the crease to go before pressing. Make sure the pieces are aligned correctly. You don't want one seam rolled over the other, or uneven corners.

4 You can use the iron to help manipulate unusual shapes. Here, I'm only pressing to crease the top portion of the bag, because this bag has a narrower opening and flares toward the bottom with rounded corners.

a word about stabilizers

The use of stabilizers in bags is of the utmost importance. These wonderful products will raise the finished quality level of your work to look very crisp and professional. Here is a breakdown of the ones that are my absolute favorites. I will be referring to them in my materials lists, so refer back to this information to understand the differences between them and why I use certain ones for particular functions.

PELLON PELTEX 7 1: This is a heavy one-sided fusible product, 20" wide and sold by the yard. I frequently use it for the exteriors of my bags so that they have body, making them stand quite nicely on their own. This product is surprisingly easy to sew through along with layers of fabric and even some other stabilizers thrown in. It responds well to intentional pressing, allowing itself to be softened and then shaped by ironing (such as for creases and corners).

PELLON FUSIBLE INTERFACING: This product is 20" wide and sold by the yard. I use the one specifically made for light- to mid-weight fabrics. It is fusible on one side. Quite often I use this stabilizer doubled for handles and a single layer on the wrong side of fabric for linings and pockets. It is easy to sew through and adds body to regular cotton.

PELLON FUSIBLE THERMOLAM PLUS: This product is 45" wide and sold by the yard. It is a polyester fleece product that is fusible on one side. Using fusible fleece will render a softer bag. It may stand a little on its own, but not so sturdily as it would with Peltex. Fusible fleece is machine-washable as well.

TEMPORARY ADHESIVE SPRAY: The two adhesive sprays I use most often are 505 or Sulky KK2000. These products are considered spray-on stabilizers. I use them in bag construction to add fabrics to the non-fusible side of Peltex or to temporarily hold a pocket in place rather than pinning. They help keep puckers out of fabrics when adding the lining fabric. The adhesive dissipates over a few days, negating the need to wash them out. They are also nice because they do not gum up the machine in any way. I also love to use this adhesive as a way to stick my paper patterns to bulkier stabilizers instead of pinning.

SIMPLE BAGS

I love sewing simple bags! You can move right through the sewing process and get to the showing-off part! The bags in this section are the perfect starting place if you're a beginning bag maker. If you have a little more experience, these bags are great as quick projects.

The Green Grocery Bag and Foldable Shoppers are great portable bags; they both fold up for storage. The Lunch Bucket Bag is so much more stylish than that old paper bag! With an easy-to-do drawstring closure, this bag is a snap to make and a pleasure to use. The Cross-Body Purses are perfect for the gal on the go. There is just enough room in either size for the essentials!

Three of the four projects are offered in more than one size. And there are lots of little details that let you add your own definitive style. Dig out your button and ribbon stash—you can put them to great use here!

GREEN GROCERY BAGS

The Green Grocery Bag is featured in three sizes. This design is based on my very popular Dharma Eco-Friendly Bag pattern that is now out of print. I felt that this was such an easy bag to make and so handy that I just had to add it to the book. I've updated the design by narrowing the handles on the larger sizes, changing the slope of the front opening, adding a ruffle edge to the outer pocket, as well as a convenient loop handle inside the pocket for easy carrying when the bags are folded up. The three sizes will even nest inside one another for additional carrying convenience.

my initial sketch

Be creative with your fabric choices. You might want to make them from a sturdy canvas or be thrifty and use an old sheet or men's size shirt. This would be the ultimate in recycling!

materials list

Fabric

Fabric A—bag exterior

   Small: ⅝ yard

   Medium: ⅔ yard

   Large: 1½ yards (this will yield leftover fabric for making another smaller bag)

Fabric B—bag lining & pocket

   Small: ⅞ yard

   Medium: 1 yard

   Large: 1½ yards

Fabric C—handle loop

   All Sizes: One 2"×14" strip

All yardage based on 45"-wide cotton fabrics.

Other Materials

Rotary cutter, ruler and mat

Sharp, pointed scissors

Removable marking pencil

Thread to match fabrics

One package of ⅜"-wide elastic

Safety pin or bodkin

Finished dimensions of the bag:

Small: 11"×10½"×5½" *deep, without the handle*
Dimensions of the bag folded: 6½"×4½"

Medium: 14½"×12½"×7½ *deep, without the handle*
Dimensions of the bag folded: 7¾"×6"

Large (shown at left): 18½"×16"×7½" *deep, without the handle*
Dimensions of the bag folded: 10"×7"

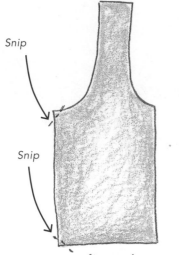

Snip

Snip

figure 1

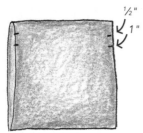

½"

1"

figure 2

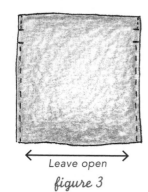

← Leave open →

figure 3

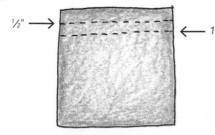

½" →

← 1"

figure 4

LAYOUT & CUTTING

The only pattern piece provided is for the Main Bag Body piece (sheet 1). The rest of the pieces are cut by measurements given in the instructions using a rotary cutter, ruler and mat. Since the sizes are nested on the pattern piece, you may want to trace the pattern for the size you want to make.

Instead of cutting the exterior bag body and lining pieces on the off-the-bolt (lengthwise) fold, I recommend you open out the fabric and then fold the selvedge edge over just enough to fit the pattern piece. For the Large Bag, fold over one selvedge edge lengthwise toward the center about 26 inches. Place the fold line of the pattern along the folded fabric edge. Pin and cut. The two exterior bag body pieces (and the two lining pieces) will be cut one below the other. You will end up with a long strip of leftover fabric, which can be used for the pocket (lining fabric), the loop handle (exterior or lining fabric) or for a Small Bag or another project. For the Small and Medium Bags, open out the fabric and fold both selvedge edges to meet at the off-the-bolt center fold-line, creating two folded edges, one on each side. Cut the two exterior bag body pieces (and the two lining pieces) side-by-side, placing the fold line of the pattern pieces along the folded edges of the fabric.

CONSTRUCTION

1   While one of the exterior bag pieces is still folded along the fold line, snip a tiny triangle on the upper and lower edge of the fold. (figure 1) This will be your front exterior panel.

2   For the pocket, cut a rectangle measuring as follows for each bag:
Large: 11½"wide × 22" long
Medium: 9½" wide × 18" long
Small: 7¾" wide × 15¼" long

3   Fold the pocket piece in half crosswise, right sides together with raw edges even and press. Measure ½" from the fold and mark on either side with a removable marking pencil. Measure 1" down from the fold and repeat. (figure 2)

4   Stitch along both sides using a ¼" seam allowance, leaving the space between the marks open for the elastic casing. Backstitch to reinforce the opening. Leave the bottom open for turning. (figure 3)

5   Clip the corners, then turn pocket right-side out and press flat, turning under the raw edges of the casing. Mark ½" and 1" down from the fold on both sides, then stitch along both lines to create the casing. (figure 4)

6 Using a long stitch length on the machine, stitch two lines of gathering stitches, ¼" and ⅜" away from the open bottom edge of the pocket. (figure 5)

7 Fold the pocket in half lengthwise and snip the center along the bottom edge (figure 6), careful not to cut through gathering threads.

8 Cut a piece of elastic for the casing as follows:
Large: 7"
Medium: 5½"
Small: 4½"

9 Attach a safety pin or bodkin to one end of elastic and pull through the casing, just until the edge of the elastic is inside the casing. Stitch across the end, ⅛" from the edge. Finish pulling the elastic through and stitch across other end. (figure 7)

10 On the outside of the bag's front piece (the one with the bottom snipped to mark the center), measure from the center snip as follows, and mark with a removable marking pencil:
Large: 3½" to either side of center
Medium: 2¾" to either side of center
Small: 2¼" to either side of center

11 Starting at these new marks, align the horizontal line of a rotary-cutting ruler with the bottom edge of the bag. Using a removable marking pencil, draw a straight line *up* on each side. (figure 8) The length of the lines for each size is as follows:
Large: 11"
Medium: 9"
Small: 7⅝"

12 To make the loop handle, fold the 2" × 14" strip in half lengthwise with wrong sides together and press. Open out the strip and fold the outer raw edges toward the center and press. Fold closed once more and edgestitch both long finished edges.

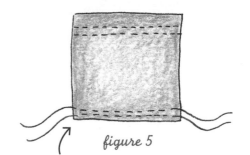

figure 5

Gathering stitches

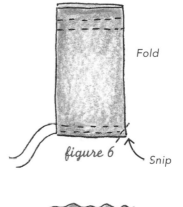

Fold

figure 6

Snip

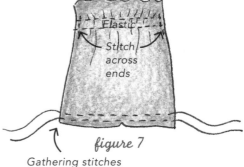

Elastic

Stitch across ends

figure 7

Gathering stitches

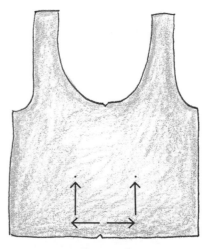

figure 8

½"   *figure 9*

Place Pocket between markings
figure 10

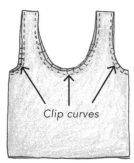

Clip curves

figure 11

Handle ends

Like fabrics together
figure 12

Bag side—like fabrics together
figure 13

13 Fold the loop handle in half so that the raw ends are together. Place it on the bag front, ½" in from either pocket side marking. (figure 9) Pin with all raw edges even and stitch across the handle ends, ¼" in from the edge.

14 Pin the pocket to the bag front, lining up the center snips and have the finished edges of pocket along vertical marks. (figure 10) Once the pocket is pinned in place, pull the gathering threads along the bottom of the pocket to make it fit within the markings. Press the pocket flat. Starting at a top corner, edge-stitch down the side, across the bottom, and up the other side. Backstitch at the beginning and ending of the pocket stitching.

15 Place one lining piece on top of each exterior piece, right sides together. Pin the large "U" shape in the center together, as well as the curved edges on either side. Stitch together with ¼" seam allowance, then clip the curves to ease the seam when turned and pressed. (figure 11) Turn one of the sections right-side out. Do not sew the sides and bottom.

16 Place the handles of the right-side out joined piece inside the handles of the joined piece that is still wrong-side out, matching exterior fabric to exterior fabric and lining fabric to lining fabric. Match up seams and all raw edges. (figure 12)

17 Pin raw edges together and then stitch with a ¼" seam allowance across each of the two open handle ends. Turn bag right side out.

18 Lay the bag flat (as shown in figure 14). Press the seams of the large center opening, the side curved edges of the handles and the handle seams flat.

19 To sew the sides of the bag: With right sides together (figure 13), pin then sew the front exterior piece to the back exterior piece along each side with ¼" seam allowance, matching the handle seams. Pin and sew the lining pieces together the same way.

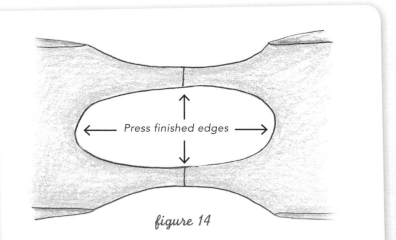

Press finished edges

figure 14

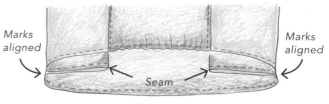

Medium Bag

Small Bag

20 Turn the bag right-side out and press the seam flat. Turn the lining to the inside of the bag and match up the side seams of the exterior and lining pieces. Pin the exterior and lining pieces together, with right sides facing outward and wrong sides against each other, with raw edges even along the bottom of the bag. Stitch around the bottom of the bag to hold the two layers of fabric together. (figure 15) *Do not* sew the bottom of the bag closed yet—you'll do that in the next step.

21 At the bottom edge of the bag, measure to either side of the side seams on the lining side and mark (figure 16):
Large: 3¾"
Medium: 3¾"
Small: 2¾"

22 Bring these two marks together to form the pleat at the bottom of the bag on each side. Start at the marks and stitch all the way across the pleat, ¼" in from the raw, lower edge. (figure 17)

Stitch around lower edges

figure 15

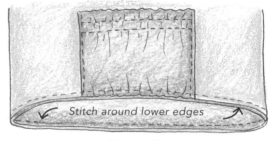

Mark lining along both side seams

figure 16

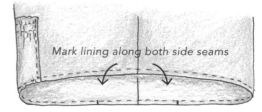

Marks aligned

Marks aligned

Seam

figure 17

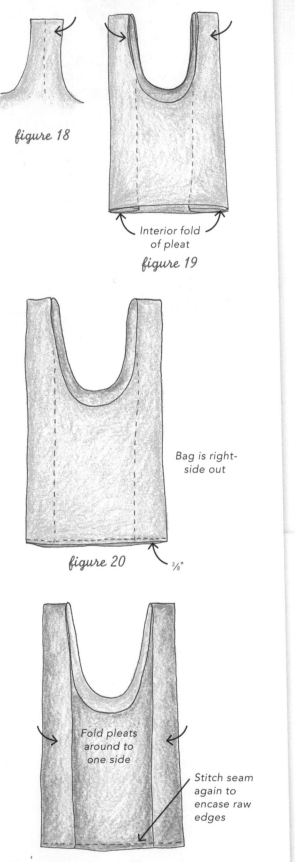

figure 18

Interior fold
of pleat

figure 19

Bag is right-
side out

figure 20   ⅜"

Fold pleats
around to
one side

Stitch seam
again to
encase raw
edges

figure 21

22 Lay the bag out flat with the bottom edges even. From the top of the handle, fold the width of the handle in *half* to the inside. (figures 18, 19) This will move the side seam of the bag to the inside, completing the pleat that was formed in the previous step. Press along the sides to form the creases of the pleat. (figure 20)

23 Sew across the bottom of the bag (right side facing out), about ⅜" from the bottom raw edge. Trim down the seam close to the stitching.

24 Now turn the bag *wrong* side out. The fold of the pleats will fall to one side of the bag. Make sure that the fold on both sides falls to the same side. I usually plan for that to be the side opposite the outer pocket. Be sure that the corners are turned completely. Press the bag flat. Sew a ½" seam across the bottom of the bag to enclose the raw edges of the seam. (figure 21) This forms a French seam and now the raw edges cannot be seen from either side of the bag!

25 Turn the bag right-side out once more and check the bottom to be sure that the entire raw edge was enclosed. Press.

26 Finish the bag by edgestitching the main opening and handles (open the handles out to do this stitching). Stitch again approximately ¼" away from the edge for decorative topstitching. (figure 22) Fold handles in half again along pressed edge and stitch the handle together through all thicknesses, using the seam as a guide.

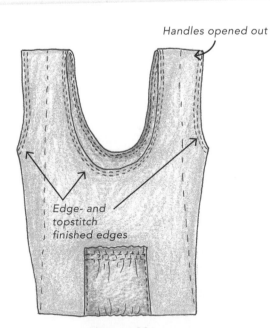

Handles opened out

Edge- and
topstitch
finished edges

figure 22

folding instructions

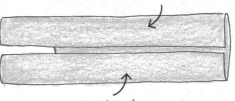
step 1

1 Turn the bag so that the side with the pocket is facing downward. Fold over each side to be even with the edge of the pocket.

2 Fold the handles over by about one-third.

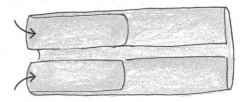
step 2

3 Fold over again so that the fold is about even with the top of the pocket

4 Carefully flip the bag over so that the pocket faces up and the bag is still folded.

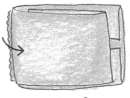
step 3

5 Slide your hand inside the pocket and grasp the folded parts of the bag. With your other hand, turn the pocket wrong side out, encasing the folded parts of the bag inside the pocket. Use your fingers to poke out the corners. Pat the bag to get it to lie flat and pull out the loop handle. When you are ready to use your bag, simply turn out the pocket again and the bag will open up.

step 4

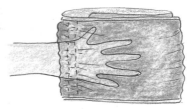
step 5

LUNCH BUCKET BAG

What a stylish way to carry your lunch! This little bag is a modern twist on the old-fashioned "lunch pail" from long ago. Featuring decorative hardware on the handle and a convenient drawstring closure, this bag is not only functional, but good-looking and easy to make. Once you carry this little number to work, everyone will want one!

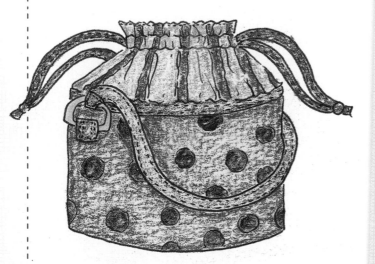

my initial sketch

Make this bag your own with a funky choice of fabrics. This is the perfect opportunity to use all of those cool food prints. Another great idea is to use laminated (vinyl-coated) cotton for the liner so that any spills or moisture can be easily wiped away. (See page 41 for tips on working with laminates.)

materials list

Fabric

Fabric A—bag exterior & handle:
⅝ yard (⅞ yard if using laminated cotton)

Fabric B—lining, binding & drawstring:
⅝ yard (¼ yard if using laminated cotton)

Fabric C—drawstring section for top of bag: ½ yard

All yardage is based on 45" wide cotton fabrics.

Other Materials

One-sided fusible stabilizer (Peltex 71): ¾ yard

Fusible interfacing for light- to mid-weight fabrics: 1 yard

Two 1¼" rings for handle (can be rectangular or circular, though the latter may require extra stitching to secure)

Rotary cutter, ruler and mat

Sharp, pointed scissors

Removable marking pencil

Heavy-duty machine needle (such as for denim)

Thread to match fabrics

Large safety pin (or bodkin)

Finished Dimensions of the Bag

10" (counting the drawstring unit) × 7", without the handle

The handle has an 8" drop.

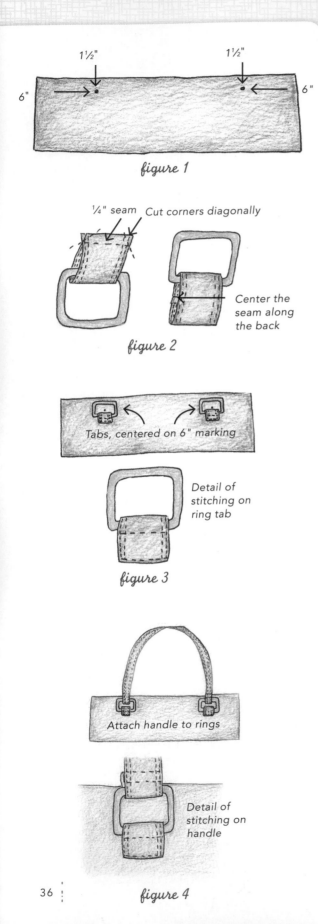

1½"   1½"

6"   6"

figure 1

¼" seam   Cut corners diagonally

Center the
seam along
the back

figure 2

Tabs, centered on 6" marking

Detail of
stitching on
ring tab

figure 3

Attach handle to rings

Detail of
stitching on
handle

figure 4

LAYOUT & CUTTING

The only pattern piece provided for this bag is the circular Bag Base (sheet 2). The rest of the pieces should be cut according to the measurements provided using a rotary cutter, ruler and mat.

MAIN BAG & HANDLES

1 Using the Circular Base pattern piece, cut one base each from Peltex and Fabric A; transfer all markings. Fuse the Peltex to the Fabric A piece (fusible side of Peltex to wrong side of fabric). Set the base aside until Step 10.

2 For the main body of the bag, cut one 6½"×24" rectangle from the Peltex and one from Fabric A. The design motif should run parallel to the short edge. Fuse Peltex to the wrong side of the rectangle. On the fabric side of the rectangle, mark the ring tab placement. Measure in 6" from either end and down 1½" from top edge, and mark. (figure 1)

3 For the handles, cut two strips—2¼" × the width of the fabric—from Fabric A. Cut three 2¼"×20" strips from interfacing; cut one in half crosswise. Apply the interfacing strips to the wrong side of the fabric strips, overlapping the interfacing strips by ¼" to piece.

4 Follow the instructions in Essential Techniques for Making Handles (pages 16–17).

5 Trim the handles down to 30". Cut two 3" lengths from the leftover pieces for the ring tabs.

6 Place the ring tab through the ring and fold in half. Sew across the end with a ¼" seam allowance. Trim the corners diagonally and position the seam at the center of the back side of the tab. Press seam flat and to one side. (figure 2)

7 Center the tabs on the 6" mark, with the top of the tab at the 1½" mark. Sew across the lower edge of the tab, then pivot and stitch up the side to just below the ring. Pivot again and stitch just below the ring (don't stitch *too* closely to the metal or you will break the needle). Pivot once more and stitch back to the beginning. Backstitch when you reach the start of the stitching. (figure 3) If you're using circular rings, sew again over the stitching under the ring for more stability.

8 To add the handle to the rings, place one end through a ring from the front. Fold the cut end over ¼", and then turn that end up by an inch or so (take care not to twist the handle). Stitch in place in the same manner as the ring tab in step 7. Repeat for the other end of the handle. (figure 4)

9 With right sides together, stitch the ends of the rectangle piece together with a ¼" seam allowance to create the main bag piece. (figure 5) Press the seam open. Fold the bag flat with the seam along one side and mark the opposite side at the top and bottom edges. Now open the bag out and align the marks just made with the seam and mark the opposite ends the same way. This divides the bag evenly into quarters, to be used later. (figure 6)

10 Divide the bag's base into quarters by folding the circle in half and snipping each end to mark. Open it out and fold in half the other direction (aligning your previous snips), then snip at each end to mark. (figure 7)

11 Complete a series of ¼" deep snips along the entire bottom edge of the main bag piece and the base. (figure 8) With right sides together, pin the main bag piece and bag base together with the wrong sides out, aligning the quarter marks. Allow the snips to ease the two pieces together. Pin fairly close together and then stitch around the bottom of the bag with a ¼"–⅜" seam allowance. (figure 9)

12 Press the bag briefly so that the steam will soften the Peltex then turn the bag right-side out. Press along the bottom seam to smooth the main bag piece. A wadded-up tea towel held inside the bag while pressing will help shape the bag and also protect your hand from the steam. Refer to the Essential Techniques section (page 22) for more details on pressing.

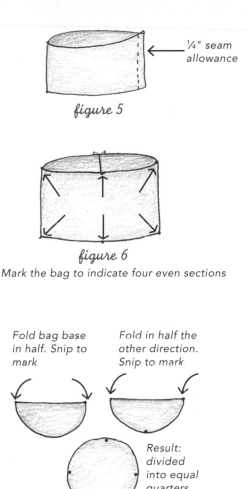

¼" seam allowance

figure 5

figure 6

Mark the bag to indicate four even sections

Fold bag base in half. Snip to mark

Fold in half the other direction. Snip to mark

Result: divided into equal quarters

figure 7

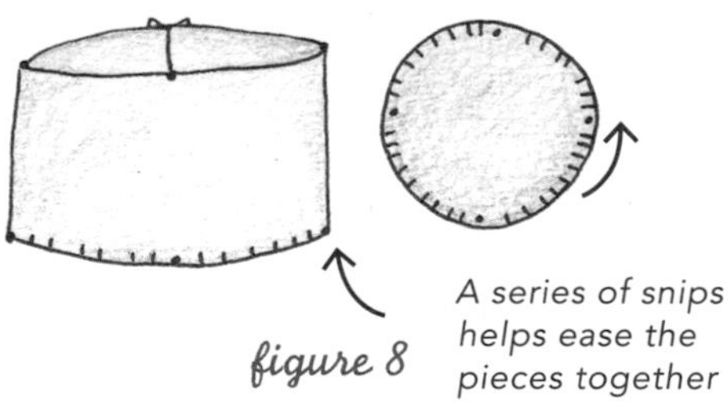

A series of snips helps ease the pieces together

figure 8

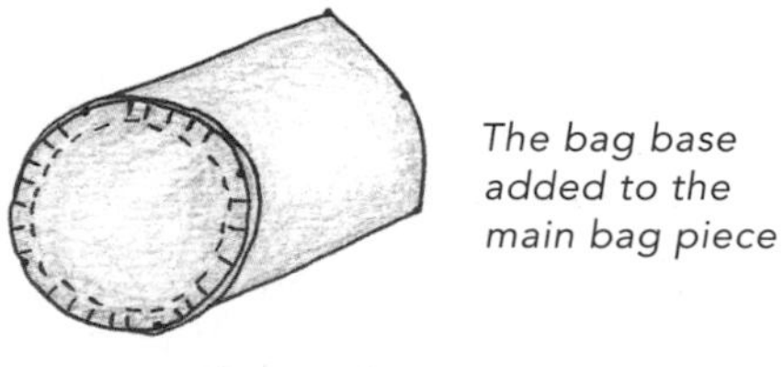

The bag base added to the main bag piece

figure 9

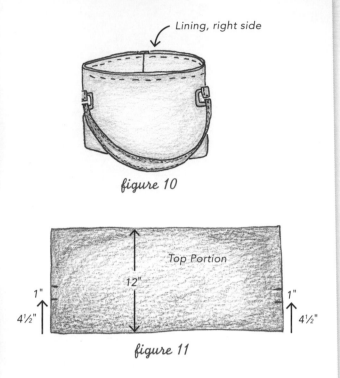

Lining, right side

figure 10

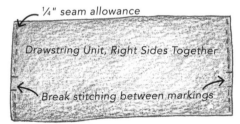

Top Portion

12"

1"

1"

4½"

4½"

figure 11

Drawstring Unit, Right Sides Together

¼" seam allowance

Break stitching between markings

figure 12

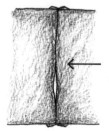

Edgestitch around opening

figure 13

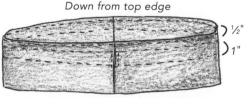

Down from top edge

½"

1"

figure 14

LINING, DRAWSTRING & BINDING

1 For the lining, follow Steps 1 and 2 on page 36, cutting from fabric B and interfacing (not Peltex). Apply the interfacing to the wrong side of the fabric.

2 Sew the side seam of the bag lining with a ⅜" seam allowance. This larger seam allowance accounts for the bulk of the Peltex, making the pieces fit together better.

3 Refer to Steps 9–11 on page 37 to assemble lining, except here, use a ⅜" seam allowance.

4 Leaving the lining wrong-side out, place it inside the main bag. This will put the wrong sides of the bag and lining together. Line up the quarter markings and pin the bag and lining together. Trim any uneven edges. Stitch around the top of the bag, ¼" from the top edge. (figure 10)

5 To make the drawstring unit of the bag, cut two 12"×18" rectangles from fabric C. The direction of design motif should run parallel to the short edge.

6 Mark on the wrong side of fabric so the markings face up when sewn. Along the 12" edge, mark 4½" up from the bottom, and again 1" above that. Repeat on the other 12" edge. This will mark the drawstring opening. (figure 11)

7 Place the two rectangles for the top portion right sides together matching raw edges and making sure design motifs run in the same direction. Sew with a ¼" seam along one side, backstitching at the first mark. Skip the 1" section. Continue the remainder of the seam from the second mark. Repeat for the other side. (figure 12)

8 Press the seams open and turn right-side out into a circular shape. Edgestitch around each opening to reinforce it. (figure 13)

9 Fold the drawstring unit in half, wrong sides together with bottom raw edges even and the openings on the *outside* of the folded piece. Press. From the top folded edge, measure down ½" and mark. Mark again 1" below that. Repeat the marks on the other side, and then draw a line with removable marking pencil. (figure 14) This will create the casing for the drawstring. Edgestitch along the top folded edge, then stitch along the ½" marked line and the 1" mark.

10 Divide the drawstring section into equal quarters (see Steps 9 and 10 on page 37). To create gathering stitches, complete two rows of stitching, using a long straight machine stitch, ¼" and ⅜" from the edge. Break stitching at each seam. (figure 15)

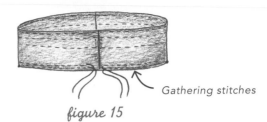

Gathering stitches

figure 15

11 Pin the drawstring unit to the inside of the bag; make sure the side with the openings is facing *away* from the lining. Pull the gathering threads until the drawstring section matches the bag opening in size. Distribute the gathers evenly and pin the lining to the bag. Stitch along the top of the bag, ⅜" from the edge. Trim the seam to ¼." (figure 16)

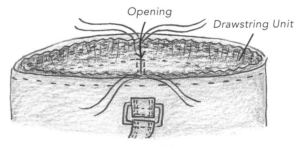

Opening *Drawstring Unit*

figure 16

12 For the binding, cut a 2¾" strip × the width of fabric from Fabric B. Trim away the selvedges and press in ½" to the wrong side on one narrow end. Fold the strip in half lengthwise, wrong sides together, and press.

13 Starting with the pressed-under edge, place the binding against the drawstring section on the inside of the bag. Pin in place until reaching the pressed end. Allow for a 1" overlap and trim away excess. Open up the pressed end and tuck the cut end inside. Close and pin in place. Stitch around the top of the bag with a ⅜" seam allowance. (figure 17)

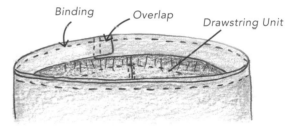

Binding *Overlap* *Drawstring Unit*

figure 17

14 Open out the binding away from the bag and press. Fold the binding down over the bag's top edge. Edgestitch the binding in place along the lower pressed edge. (figure 18)

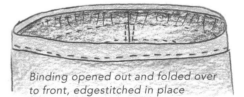

Binding opened out and folded over to front, edgestitched in place

figure 18

15 Open out the drawstring unit from the inside of the bag and press. Stitch through all thicknesses at the upper finished edge of the binding to secure the drawstring section to the upper exterior of the bag. (figure 19)

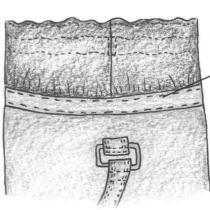

Drawstring unit, opened out

Stitch along finished edge of binding to secure drawstring unit to upper edge of bag.

figure 19

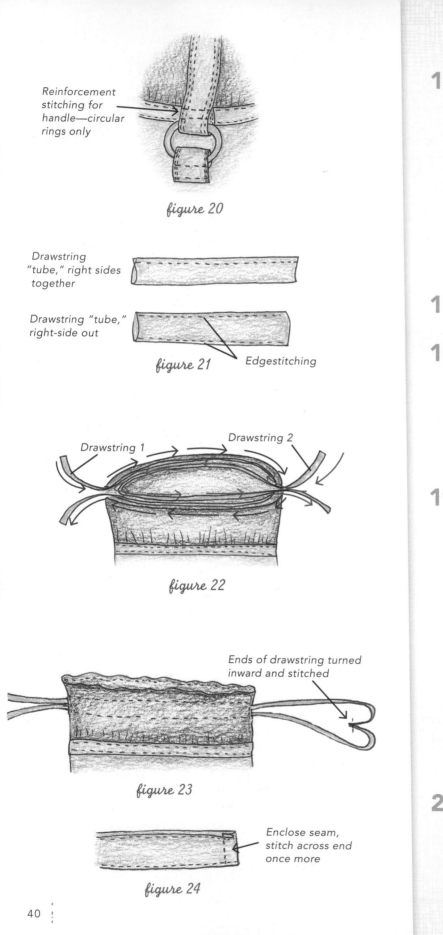

Reinforcement stitching for handle—circular rings only

figure 20

Drawstring "tube," right sides together

Drawstring "tube," right-side out

Edgestitching

figure 21

Drawstring 1   Drawstring 2

figure 22

Ends of drawstring turned inward and stitched

figure 23

Enclose seam, stitch across end once more

figure 24

16 If you used circular rings, the bag may have a tendency to tip. To prevent this, place the handle over the binding directly opposite the ring and tab and stitch through all thicknesses (including the handle) along the previous stitching at the top edge of the binding. (figure 20) This will make the handle stationary. You can also do this with a square ring, but it may not be necessary. The bag on page 34 shows the reinforced stitching; the variation using laminated cotton on the facing page does not.

17 Cut two 2"×27" strips from Fabric B for the drawstrings.

18 Trim away the selvedges and fold in half lengthwise, right sides together. Stitch along the long edges with a ¼" seam allowance, forming a tube. Repeat with the second strip. Turn the tubes right-side out and, with the seam along one side, press. Edgestitch along each edge. (figure 21)

19 Pin a large safety pin through one end of one of the drawstrings. Insert pinned end into one of the openings in the drawstring casing. Pull the drawstring all the way around until you reach the opening where you started; pull the end through. Remove the safety pin. Attach the safety pin to the remaining drawstring, insert through the opposite opening and draw through the casing the same way. There should be two ends coming out of each opening. Test to see that they were properly threaded by pulling all the ends at the same time. This should result in the bag pulling closed. If not, then the drawstrings are not correctly inserted. (figure 22)

20 Open the bag fully. With the ends of the drawstrings together and folded inward as shown in the illustration, stitch them together with a ⅛" seam (figure 23). With the seam inward, stitch across the end again, encasing the seams (figure 24). Tie a knot close to the stitched ends.

Laminated Cotton

This is the perfect bag for trying out the new laminated cottons on the market! Laminated cotton is so cute for the outside... and so smart for the lining! Leaky containers aren't such a big deal if you can just wipe up the spills! You'll just need to adapt the yardage listed for the project, because the typical fabric width for laminated cotton is 56" to 58", rather than 44".

To make the exterior bag, liner and handle from laminated cotton, cut both rectangles for the lower portion of the bag (exterior and lining) from this fabric, as well as the handle strips and circular base. You'll need ⅞ yard of laminated cotton, since this will be both Fabric A and the lining portion of Fabric B. You'll only need a ¼ yard of Fabric B (for binding and drawstring) for this variation.

If you do decide to try out the laminated cottons, there are a few sewing tips I have for you. Because the vinyl coating can melt when direct heat is applied, use a tea towel or press cloth between the iron and the vinyl coating. This allows you to smooth out wrinkles without melting the vinyl.

You may also want to think about purchasing an additional sewing machine foot. Regular machine feet have a tendency to drag on the vinyl, preventing the fabric from feeding through the machine properly. Some sewing machine manufacturers make a special machine foot designed to work with vinyls. I've found that a Teflon foot works well; it helps the fabric flow smoothly under the needle.

If you have trouble finding a laminated cotton that you like, try an iron-on vinyl (such as Heat-n-Bond). This product can be ironed onto your fabric, making it water-resistant. It's sold by the roll or yard, and is usually 17" wide. Just follow the manufacturer's instructions, and you'll have custom-laminated fabric.

FOLDABLE SHOPPERS

The Foldable Shoppers, featured in two fabrics and sizes, are a great way to shop in an eco-friendly way. Take these bags everywhere you go whenever you know that treasures will be brought home with you. They are easily portable since they fold up and stay that way with a button and loop closure. There is even an exterior pocket that is accessible while the bags are closed, perfect for stashing little extras! These are so quick and easy you will find yourself making more than one of each size!

my initial sketch

How about using laminated cotton or a home decorating fabric for this bag? If you use heavier fabrics, you may not need the interfacing in the body of the bag. Another option is to piece some scraps together before cutting the outer bag rectangles. Not only would the scrappy look be cute, but it would recycle all those extra pieces! How green can you get?

materials list

Fabric

Fabric A—bag exterior, lining & pocket

Medium: 1¼ yards

Large: 1⅝ yards (lining will be pieced)

Fabric B—handles & pocket trim

Medium: ⅜ yard

Large: ½ yard

Other Materials

Fusible interfacing for light- to mid-weight fabrics:

Medium: 1⅞ yards

Large: 2½ yards

Rotary cutter, ruler and mat

Removable marking pencil

Sharp, pointed scissors

Thread to match fabrics

½ yard ribbon

1 decorative button

Finished Dimensions

Medium: 12"×18"×6" deep, without the handle. The handle has a 9" drop. Dimensions of the bag folded: 6½"×8"

Large: 14"×21"×8" deep, without the handle. The handle has a 10" drop. Dimensions of the bag folded: 7½"×9"

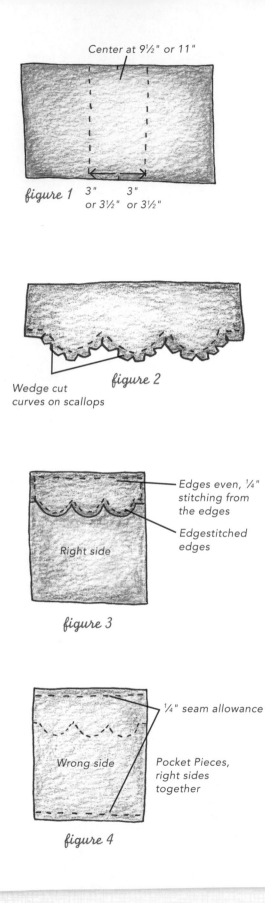

Center at 9½" or 11"

figure 1   3"   3"
          or 3½"   or 3½"

Wedge cut
curves on scallops

figure 2

Edges even, ¼"
stitching from
the edges

Edgestitched
edges

Right side

figure 3

¼" seam allowance

Wrong side

Pocket Pieces,
right sides
together

figure 4

LAYOUT & CUTTING

The only pattern piece provided for these bags is the scallop trim for the pocket (medium on sheet 3, large on sheet 5). The rest of the pieces are cut by measurements given in the instructions using a rotary cutter, ruler and mat.

MAIN BAG & POCKET

1 Cut four rectangles from Fabric A.
Medium: 19"×16"
Large: 22"×19"
The direction of fabric's design motif should run parallel to the smaller edge for each size.

2 Cut two pieces of fusible interfacing same size as fabric A. Apply to the wrong side of two of the fabric A pieces. These will form the exterior of the bag. Set the remaining two rectangles aside.

3 With the fabric side of the interfaced pieces facing up, mark the center at the top and bottom edges. (figure 1)
Medium: Center at 9½", then 3" to either side of center
Large: Center at 11", then 3½" to either side of center

4 For the pocket, cut two rectangles from Fabric A and one from fusible interfacing.
Medium: 6"×7"
Large: 7"×8"
The direction of the design motif should run parallel to the longer edge.

5 Using the Pocket Scallop Trim pattern piece in the appropriate size, cut two pieces from Fabric B and one from fusible interfacing, transferring all pattern markings. Apply interfacing to the wrong side of one scalloped piece and one rectangle from Step 4.

6 Place the scalloped trim pieces right sides together and stitch along the scalloped edge with a ⅜" seam allowance. Wedge cut notches in the curves of the scallops and snip closely to the seam allowance at the points before turning. (figure 2)

7 Turn trim right-side out and fully turn out the scallops. Press. Edgestitch the scalloped edge. Pin the trim to right side the interfaced pocket piece from Step 5, along the top edge. Keep the side and top edges even. Stitch together, ¼" in from the edges. (figure 3)

8 Place the remaining pocket piece from Step 4 on top of the scalloped one, right-sides together. Stitch along the top and bottom edges with a ¼" seam allowance. (figure 4)

9 Turn the pocket right-side out and press along the top and bottom edges. Edgestitch along the top edge of the pocket. Fold the pocket in half lengthwise and mark the bottom edge for the center. (figure 5)

10 Pin the pocket to the right side of one of the interfaced exterior bag pieces.
Medium: 3½" up from the bottom and centered on the 9½" marking
Large: 4½" up from the bottom and centered on the 11" marking.
Stitch the sides and bottom edge of the pocket in place. (figure 6)

HANDLES

1 For the handles, cut strips that are 2¼" wide by the width of fabric in these quantities:
Medium: cut five strips
Large: cut six strips
Trim off the selvedges.

2 For Medium, cut the fifth strip into four equal pieces and sew one of these to each of the remaining four strips, right-sides together, with a ¼" seam. Press seams open. Trim the four strips to 50".

For Large, cut two of the strips in half and sew one to each of the remaining four strips, right-sides together, with a ¼" seam. Press seams open. Trim the strips to 58".

3 Cut 2¼" wide strips from interfacing and apply to the wrong side of two of the handle strips, overlapping by ¼" as necessary.
Medium: cut ten strips
Large: cut twelve strips

4 Follow the steps in Essential Techniques for creating the handles (pages 16–17).

5 Place the handles on the exterior bag pieces, centered at the outside pocket markings; they should cover the raw edges of the pocket. The raw edges of the handles should be even with the bag's bottom edge. Make sure the handle is not twisted, then pin in place. Mark 2" down from the top (on either side of the handle on the bag itself). This is where the edgestitching will turn and go across the handle. (figure 7)

6 Begin edgestitching the handle at the lower edge of the bag, following the previous edgestitching on the handle. Pivot at the 2" marking, backstitch across the handle, then continue down the other side. (figure 7) Repeat for the three remaining handle ends.

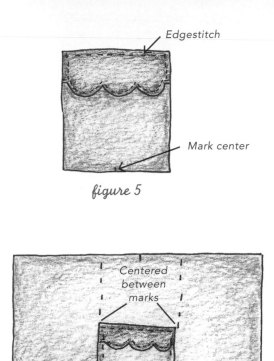

figure 5

Edgestitch

Mark center

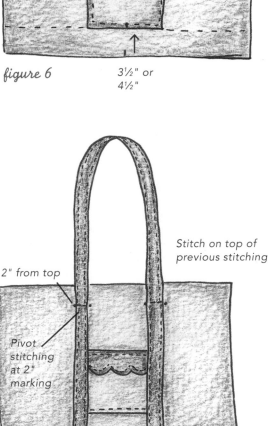

figure 6

3½" or 4½"

Centered between marks

2" from top

Pivot stitching at 2" marking

Stitch on top of previous stitching

Handle centered on 3" marking

figure 7

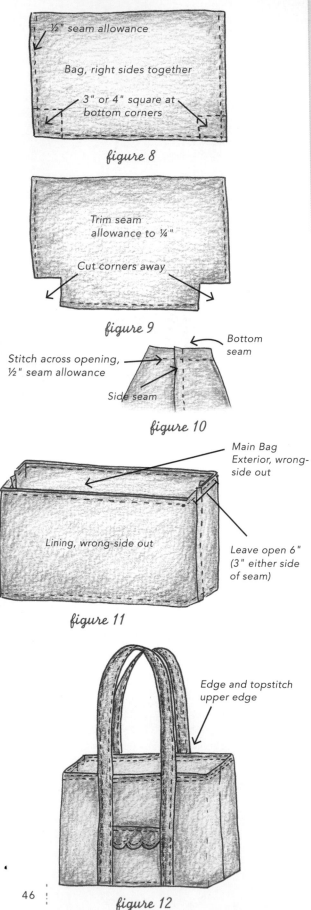

½" seam allowance

Bag, right sides together

3" or 4" square at bottom corners

figure 8

Trim seam allowance to ¼"

Cut corners away

figure 9

Bottom seam

Stitch across opening, ½" seam allowance

Side seam

figure 10

Main Bag Exterior, wrong-side out

Lining, wrong-side out

Leave open 6" (3" either side of seam)

figure 11

Edge and topstitch upper edge

figure 12

SEW THE OUTER BAG TOGETHER

1 Place the outer bag pieces right sides together, matching up side and bottom edges. Pin then sew together with a ½" seam allowance. Mark a 3" or 4" square at each bottom corner, including the seam allowance in the measurement (figure 8). *Medium*: 3" square; *Large*: 4" square

2 Cut away the corners on the marked lines. Trim down the seam allowances to ¼". (figure 9)

3 To form the corners for the bag, bring the bottom seam and side seams together, right sides together; pin. Stitch across this edge with a ½" seam allowance. (figure 10) Trim down the seam to ¼". Press seams flat.

MAKE THE LINING AND FINISH THE BAG

1 Use the remaining two rectangles from Step 1 on page 44 and sew them together following Steps 1–3 of Sewing the Outer Bag Together, above.

2 With the lining wrong-side out, place the main bag inside, with right sides of the exterior and lining together. Make sure the handles are tucked between the two layers. Match up the side seams and the centers; pin. Stitch together with a ½" seam allowance, leaving a 6" opening along one side (3" to either side of one of the side seams). (figure 11)

3 Turn the bag right-side out through the 6" opening. Turn the lining to the inside of the bag and press along the top seam. Then fully press the bag so that all layers and seams lie together smoothly. Turn the edges of the 6" opening under ½" and edgestitch all the way around the top edge; stitch again ¼" from edgestitching. (figure 12)

4 To hold all of the layers in place, slip the bag under the machine and stitch through all thicknesses, following the inside stitching on the handle, turning about even with the bottom corners of the bag. (figure 13)

figure 13

5   To fold the bag, first turn it pocket-side down. Fold the bottom in along the angled corner seams and the handles down toward the bag. (figure 14)

6   Fold the bag into thirds by folding each side in along the outer handle edge. (figure 15)

7   Fold the bag in half height-wise. The top edge of the bag should be even with the top edge of the pocket on the other side. Mark the center between the handles along the top edge of the bag. (figure 16)

8   Flip the bag over so that the pocket faces up. Mark the center at the lower edge of the pocket. (figure 17)

9   Open out the bag and sew a button to the top edge center marking. Cut ribbon long enough to form a loop that will accommodate the button and sew it to the center bottom of the pocket through all thicknesses. Tie a bow from the same ribbon and machine sew it in place on top of the raw edges of the ribbon loop. (figure 18)

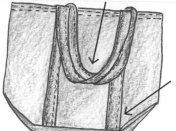

Fold down handles

Fold bottom in along corners

figure 14

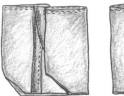

Fold in Bag Sides along handle edge

figure 15

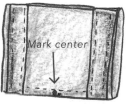

Mark center

figure 16

Mark center

figure 17

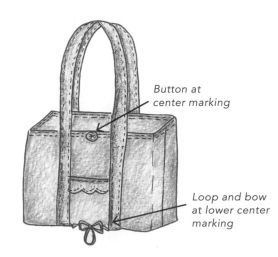

Button at center marking

Loop and bow at lower center marking

figure 18

CROSS-BODY PURSES

The Cross-Body Purse is a sweet little on-the-hip bag that's perfect for a day spent running around doing your favorite things. Offered in two sizes, these versatile bags are able to hold just a few of the essentials or a bit more, depending on your personal preferences. There are convenient interior pockets for keeping your cell phone at your fingertips, and the twist lock closure keeps everything in its place. The adjustable handle makes this purse a cinch to switch from cross-body to over the shoulder in a flash!

my initial sketch

I initially had the design more rounded, but liked the boxier final result. I also made a decision to taper the bag depth so that the opening is narrow. This makes the purse lie closer to the body for a more flattering look. Try making your cross-body purse from all one fabric; just combine the yardage requirements.

materials list

Fabric

Fabric A—bag exterior & interior pocket

  All Sizes: ½ yard

Fabric B—lining & flap

  All Sizes: ⅝ yard

Fabric C—ring tabs, binding & handles

  Small: ½ yard

  Large: ⅔ yard

Fabric yardage based on 45"-wide cotton fabrics.

Other Materials

Peltex 71 (one-sided fusible stabilizer):

  Small: ¾ yard

  Large: 1 yard

Fusible interfacing for light- to mid-weight fabrics:

  Small: ⅞ yard

  Large: 1⅝ yards

Two 1¼" D-rings

Two 1¼" swivel clasps

One 1¼" double loop slider

One ¾" twist lock

Rotary cutter, ruler and mat

Sharp, pointed scissors

Removable marking pencil

Heavy-duty machine needle (such as for denim)

Thread to match fabrics

Needle-nose pliers

Awl

Finished Dimensions

Small: 9"×7½" with a base depth of 2½"

Large: 10"×9" with a base depth of 2½"

Both bags have an adjustable 60" long handle.

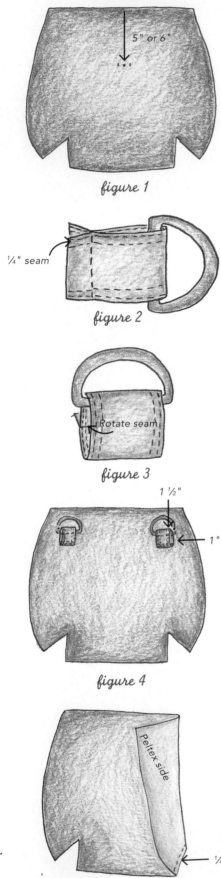

figure 1

¼" seam

figure 2

Rotate seam

figure 3

1 ½"

1"

figure 4

Peltex side

¼" seam

50

figure 5

LAYOUT & CUTTING

For this bag, you'll use these pattern pieces: Main Body (Small, sheet 3; Large, sheet 2), Purse Flap (Small, sheet 2; Large, sheet 3) and Interior Pocket (Large, sheet 1; Small, sheet 3). Make sure you cut the correct size for every piece. The ring tabs and handles will be cut by measurements given in the instructions below.

BAG EXTERIOR

1   Cut two Main Bag Body pieces each from Peltex and Fabric A. Fuse the Peltex to the wrong side of the fabric pieces.

2   On the right side of one bag piece, mark a horizontal placement line for the twist portion for the closure. Measure down from the center of the upper edge:
Small: 5"
Large: 6"
This will be the front piece of the bag body.

3   Center the twist portion of the clasp horizontally over the center mark and mark prong placement. (figure 1) Use an awl to pierce the prong marks and enlarge those holes slightly with sharp, pointed scissors. Install the twist portion of the clasp on the right side of the main bag body, following the instructions in Step 11 on page 131.

4   From Fabric C and fusible interfacing, cut two 2½"×10" strips for the ring tabs. Fuse the interfacing to the wrong side of the strips. Follow the instructions for creating handles on pages 16–17 in the Essential Techniques section to make one 10"-long strip.

5   Cut the 10" piece into two 4"-long pieces, discarding the rest. Place each 4" piece through one of the D-rings and fold in half with raw edges even. Stitch across the end with a ¼" seam. (figure 2)

6   Rotate the seam on the ring so that it is centered along one side. (figure 3)

7   On the *non-clasp* main bag body piece (the back of the bag), measure 1½" down from the top and 1" in from the side, and mark. Repeat on the other side. (figure 4)

8   Place the upper outside corner of the ring tab at this mark and stitch in place along the lower edge of the tab. Stitch another line close to the ring. Repeat for the remaining tab. (figure 4)

9   Sew the darts in the bottom corners of the front and back main body bag pieces. Fold with right sides together, aligning the angled raw edges of the dart. Stitch from the fold to the outer lower edge with a ¼" seam allowance. (figure 5)

10 Place the front and back bag pieces right sides together with all edges even and dart seams together. Stitch the bag together with a ½" seam. (figure 6) Stitch again to reinforce. It's helpful to push the darts on one half of the bag inward so that the pieces nest together when you stitch the bag together.

11 Trim down the seam and clip the curves (page 21 in Essential Techniques).

12 Briefly steam the bag to soften the Peltex, then turn right-side out and press (page 22 in the Essential Techniques).

BAG INTERIOR

1 Cut two lining pieces from both fusible interfacing and Fabric B, using the Main Body Bag pattern piece. Fuse the interfacing to the wrong side of the fabric pieces.

2 Cut two Interior Pocket pieces from both fusible interfacing and Fabric A. Fuse the interfacing to the wrong side of the fabric pieces.

3 Place the interior pocket pieces right sides together, then stitch the upper and lower edges with a ¼" seam. (figure 7) Turn the pocket right-side out and press. Edgestitch the upper edge of the pocket. (figure 8)

4 On the right side of one of the lining pieces, place and pin the pocket up from the lower edge:
Small: 3⅛"
Large: 3⅝"
Edgestitch the lower edge of the pocket in place, then stitch ¼" in from the side edges. Mark down the center of the pocket to divide it, then stitch down the marking. (figure 9)

5 Stitch the darts on the lower edges of the lining as you did for the bag exterior (step 9, page 50), then sew the two halves—right-sides together—with a ⅝" seam allowance. This slightly larger seam allowance helps reduce bulk of the Peltex and makes the exterior bag and lining pieces fit together nicely. Trim seam to ¼".

6 Place the lining inside the exterior bag with *wrong* sides together. Determine if you want the inside pocket in the front or back, and place lining accordingly.

7 Smooth the lining into place, matching the upper edges and seams. Pin the layers together, then stitch around the upper edge, ¼" from raw edges. (figure 10)

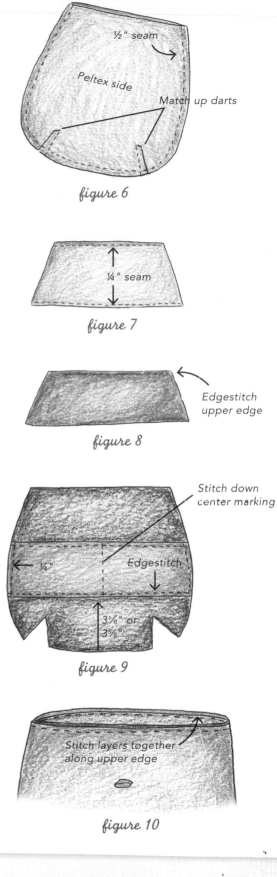

½" seam

Peltex side

Match up darts

figure 6

¼" seam

figure 7

Edgestitch upper edge

figure 8

Stitch down center marking

¼"

Edgestitch

3⅛" or 3⅝"

figure 9

Stitch layers together along upper edge

figure 10

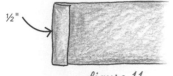
½"

figure 11

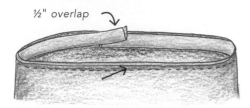
½" overlap

figure 12

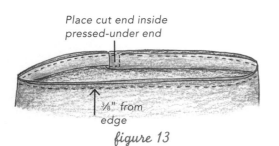
Place cut end inside
pressed-under end

⅜" from
edge

figure 13

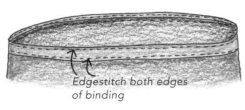
Edgestitch both edges
of binding

figure 14

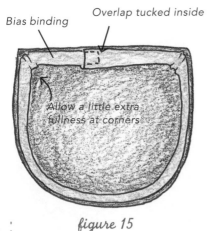
Bias binding   Overlap tucked inside

Allow a little extra
fullness at corners

figure 15

BINDING

1 To bind the top of the bag, cut a strip from Fabric C that is 2" × the width of fabric. Trim off the selvedges. Fold ½" to the wrong side along one of the narrow ends and press. (figure 11)

2 Fold the strip in half lengthwise with wrong sides together and press.

3 Starting with the pressed-under edge, place the binding strip against the lining side of the bag with raw edges even. Pin in place all the way around until you reach the pressed-under edge. Allow ½" extra and trim away the excess binding. (figure 12)

4 Open out the pressed-under end and tuck the cut end inside. Pin in place, then stitch around the top of the bag with a ⅜" seam allowance. (figure 13)

5 Fold the binding around the seam to the exterior of the bag. If the seam seems too bulky, trim it down slightly, then proceed with folding the binding to the outside. Pin in place. Edgestitch the lower folded edge. Edgestitch the upper edge to finish, then press. (figure 14)

FLAP & HANDLES

1 Using the correct Purse Flap pattern piece (Small versus Large), cut one from Peltex, and two from Fabric B. Fuse the Peltex to the wrong side of one of the flap pieces. (This will be the front of the flap.) Use temporary spray adhesive to adhere the remaining fabric piece to the non-sticky side of the Peltex with the fabric facing right-side out. (This will be the back of the flap.) Edgestitch around the outside edges to hold the layers together.

2 From the remainder of Fabric C, cut a series of 2"-wide bias strips (pages 14–15 in Essential Techniques).

3 Starting along the upper straight edge of the flap piece and beginning with the pressed-under edge, add the bias binding to the flap piece along the back. Keep the raw edges even.

4 Pin in place all the way around until you reach the beginning. Allow ½" extra and trim away the excess. Tuck the cut end inside the pressed one and pin in place. Stitch around the outer edge with a ¼" seam allowance. (figure 15)

5 Trim the corners to slightly round them, then fold and press the binding around the edge of the flap to conceal the raw edges. Edgestitch both edges of the binding in place. (figure 16)

6 Mark the center of the top (straight) edge of the flap; mark the center of the back bag exterior (side with rings) along the binding. Line up these marks with the flap binding overlapping the exterior bag binding on the exterior. The flap should be centered between the side seams.

7 Pin in place, then stitch over the edgestitching of the flap to attach. Stitch again along the previous stitching, ¼" above. (figure 17) Fold the flap over to the front side of the bag. Briefly steam the fold to crease the Peltex.

8 Add the remaining half of the twist lock to the flap by measuring up from the lower (curved) edge:
Small: 1"
Large: 1¼"

9 Mark for the prongs as before (in Steps 2 and 3, page 50) and trace around the opening of the lock onto the fabric. Carefully trim away the oval for the opening, then install the remainder of the lock the same way you installed the twist portion (Step 11, page 131).

10 Cut three strips 2½" × width of the fabric from Fabric C for the handles. Cut the third strip in half, and then sew those lengths to the two remaining strips, resulting in two long strips.

11 Cut seven 2½"-wide strips from fusible interfacing and add to the wrong side of the fabric, overlapping by ¼" as necessary.

12 Follow the instructions in Essential Techniques for Making Handles (pages 16–17), then trim them down to about 60".

13 To attach the first swivel clasp, insert the end of the handle through the loop's clasp. Fold the raw edge over twice by ½". Stitch in place along the edge, then topstitch to reinforce. Stitch and topstitch across the handle close to the loop. (figure 19)

14 Install the double loop slider and remaining swivel clasp according to the Essential Techniques section (pages 18–19). Clip the handle onto the bag. Adjust the handle as desired.

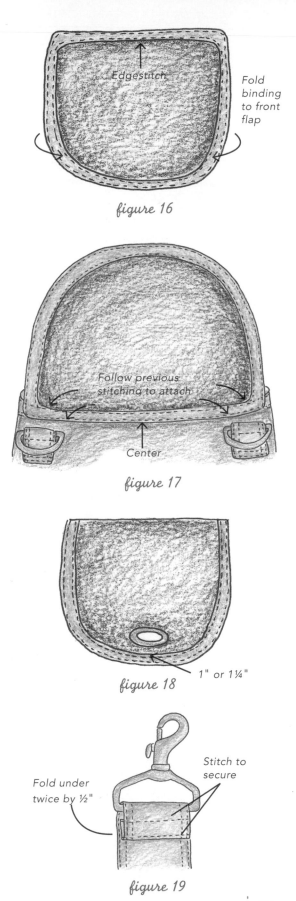

Edgestitch

Fold binding to front flap

figure 16

Follow previous stitching to attach

Center

figure 17

1" or 1¼"

figure 18

Fold under twice by ½"

Stitch to secure

figure 19

INTERMEDIATE BAGS

All of these projects build on the techniques and skills used in the Simple Bags section, but step up your bag-making skills with techniques like zipper installation, quilting your own fabrics and working with special fabric like wool and silk.

The Quilted Duffel and Tulip Tote are both soft-sided bags. While I normally like a lot of structure, I decided to show my softer side—but even these bags will remain shapely when stuffed to the top! The Versatile Handle Handbag and Ruffle Hobo have a bit more structure and detail. The Socialite Handbag is the most structured with a lovely teardrop shape.

These bags do a great job of highlighting special fabrics, so get out those favorites of yours that you have a yard or so of and get ready to showcase them! Don't forget to grab more bling—many of these bags really shine with the addition of a great zipper charm, pin or fabulous button.

QUILTED DUFFEL BAG

The Quilted Duffel bag is one of just a few soft-sided bags that I have included in this book. I usually like very structured bags—ones that stand on their own and hold their shape whether they are filled with items or not. Even though this is a soft bag, I feel that the shape of the pieces and the finishing stitching along the outer seams provide a nice structure. This design provides the perfect opportunity to use double-faced quilted fabrics. These are fabrics that are already quilted when you purchase them. It makes for a quick assembly. In the event that you cannot locate such a fabric, no worries—I've provided information about how to create your own quilted fabric!

my initial sketch

To make this bag your own, think about these other ideas: You could quilt up some laminated cotton fabric with a regular cotton for the lining. (If you choose this option, check out the sidebar on laminates on page 41) You could also make the exterior of the bag scrappy by piecing some of your favorite fabric scraps together and then quilting it. Cute embellishments such as wide ribbon or other decorative trims would give this bag a lot of personality. Let your imagination soar!

materials list

Fabrics

Fabric A—double-faced quilted fabric for main bag and end pieces: 1 yard

Fabric B—exterior pockets/zipper tabs: ⅓ yard

Fabric C—handles: ⅜ yard

Fabric D—bag bottom (interior and exterior), zipper binding, and interior seam binding: ½ yard

Other Materials

¼ yard Peltex one-sided fusible

1¼ yards fusible interfacing for light- to mid-weight fabrics

One 14" non-separating sport zipper

1 zipper charm

Removable marking pencil

Matching polyester thread

Zipper foot

Rotary cutter, ruler and mat

Sharp, pointed scissors

Temporary adhesive spray

Finished Dimensions of the bag

10½"×17½"×8" deep at base, 4" deep at top. 34"-long handles with 15" drop

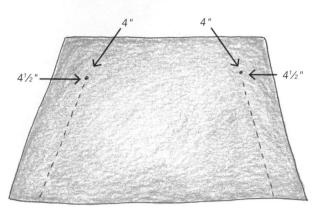

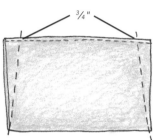

figure 1

figure 2

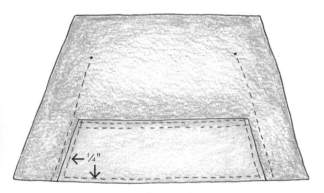

figure 3

LAYOUT & CUTTING

Pattern pieces for the Main Bag Side and End are provided on sheet 4. All other pieces are cut based on measurements provided throughout the instructions using a ruler, rotary cutter and mat.

LARGE EXTERIOR POCKETS & HANDLES

1 Using the Main Bag Side and End pattern pieces, cut out two of each from Fabric A, transferring all marks. (If you are making your own quilted fabric for Fabric A, refer to page 63.) On each piece, mark a line 4½" in from each side, stopping 4" from the top edge on each Main Bag Side piece. (figure 1)

2 For the Main Exterior Pocket, cut a 12"×9" rectangle from Fabric B and interfacing. Fuse the interfacing to the wrong side of the fabric.

3 Fold the rectangle in half *wrong*-sides together so that it measures 6"×9" and press. Edge and topstitch the top folded edge. Mark in ¾" from each top corner; line up a ruler from this marking to the bottom corner and mark. (figure 2) Cut along both lines.

4 Center this pocket along the lower edge of one Main Bag piece with the wider edge at the bottom edge of the main bag. Pin in place, then stitch ¼" in from the sides and bottom edges of the pocket to attach. (figure 3) The raw edges of the pocket will be concealed later by the handle placement and the bottom seam.
  If you desire a pocket on the other side, repeat these instructions on the other main bag piece.

5 For the handles, cut five strips 2½" wide × the width of fabric from Fabric C. Trim away the selvedges, then cut one of the strips into four equal parts. Add one of these shorter lengths to each of the other four handle strips, right sides together, with a ¼" seam allowance. Press the seam allowance open.

6 Cut twelve strips 2½" × width of the fabric from fusible interfacing and fuse to the wrong side of the handle strips, overlapping interfacing by ¼" as needed.

7 To make two handles, follow the instructions in the Essential Techniques for Making Handles (pages 16–17).

8 Once the handles have been completed, press them, then trim each one down to a length of 54". Discard the leftover pieces.

9 Place one of the handles on one of the Main Bag pieces with the outer edge of the handle along the 4½" markings made in Step 1 and the lower edges even. Pin in place. Be sure to cover the raw edges of the pocket sides with the handle placement. Take care not to twist the handle during pinning. Stop pinning at the 4" mark below the top edge. (figure 4)

10 Following the previous handle edgestitching, attach the handles. Start at the lower edge of the bag piece. Stitch up to the 4" mark, pivot and stitch across the handle to the opposite edgestitching, then pivot and stitch down. (figure 4) Repeat this stitching for the other end of the handle as well as the remaining handle and bag pieces.

BAG ENDS

1 From Fabric B and fusible interfacing, cut two rectangles, 12"×5" wide for the End Pockets.

2 Fold the rectangles in half, right-sides together, so that they measure 6"×5". Sew the side seams with a ¼" seam allowance, leaving the bottom of the pocket open. Clip the corners (figure 5), turn right-side out and press. Edge- and topstitch the upper finished edge of each pocket. (figure 6)

3 Add the pockets to each Bag End piece, centered from side to side with bottom edges even. Edgestitch the sides of the pockets and ¼" up from the bottom edge to attach. (figure 7)

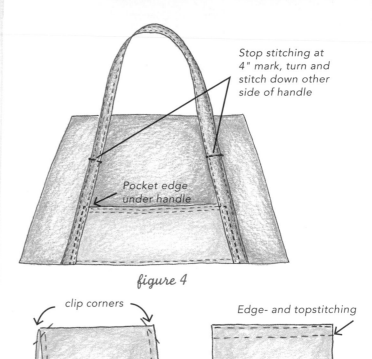

Stop stitching at 4" mark, turn and stitch down other side of handle

Pocket edge under handle

figure 4

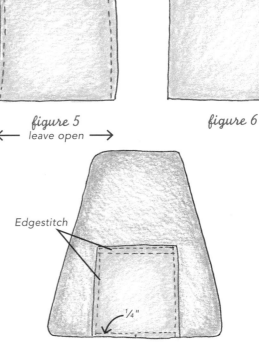

clip corners

figure 5
← *leave open* →

Edge- and topstitching

figure 6

Edgestitch

¼"

figure 7

Fussy Cutting

When cutting pieces that will be front and center, you really want to make the most of the fabric's design. Say, for example, that the fabric you chose for the exterior of a bag has a large rose motif, and you want one of the roses to appear in the center of the bag flap. When cutting the fabric, make sure that motif is perfectly framed within the measurements, or centered under the pattern piece, before cutting. This is called "fussy cutting." Some design motifs may require extra fabric yardage (¼ yard or so) to accommodate fussy cutting.

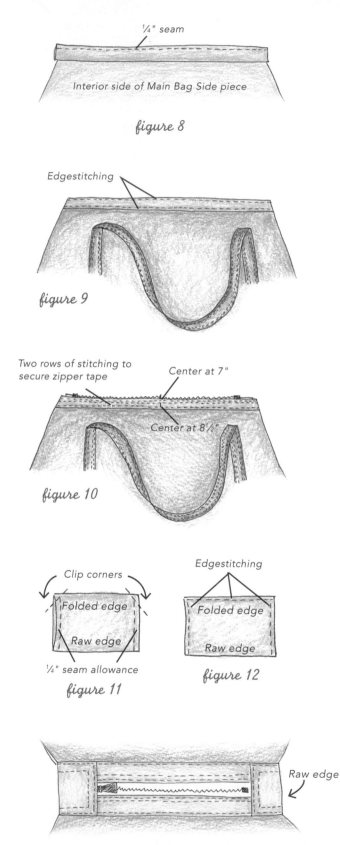

¼" seam

Interior side of Main Bag Side piece

figure 8

Edgestitching

figure 9

Two rows of stitching to secure zipper tape

Center at 7"

Center at 8½"

figure 10

Clip corners

Folded edge

Raw edge

¼" seam allowance

figure 11

Edgestitching

Folded edge

Raw edge

figure 12

Raw edge

figure 13

ADDING THE ZIPPER

1 Cut a strip 2¼" × the width of fabric from Fabric D for the zipper binding. Trim off the selvedges, then fold the strip in half lengthwise, wrong-sides together and press. Cut the strip in half for two strips approximately 22".

2 Add one strip to the interior side of each Main Bag piece along the top edge, matching raw edges. Stitch with a ¼" seam. (figure 8)

3 Open out the bindings away from the bag pieces and press the seams, then fold the binding around to the exterior side of the bag and press. Edgestitch the lower folded edge in place. (figure 9)

4 Mark the center of the zipper on the zipper tape (at 7") and the center of the top edge of the bag piece (at 8½"). Match up the center markings and pin the zipper so that the zipper tape is mostly concealed by the binding. (figure 10)

5 Use a zipper foot to attach the zipper to each Main Bag piece. Add another line of stitching along the binding about ¼" away from the edge next to the zipper. This will reinforce the stitching at the zipper. (figure 10) Zip the zipper halves together.

6 Cut two 2"×3" rectangles from Fabric D. Fold these in half, right-sides together, so that they measure 2"×1½". Stitch down the sides with a ¼" seam allowance; clip the corners. (figure 11) Turn right-side out and press, then edgestitch. (figure 12)

7 Add these pieces to the ends of the zipper to provide a neat appearance to the zipper and close the gap between the zipper end and bag edge. The outer edges of these small rectangles should line up with the outer edges of the binding. Pin in place, then edgestitch. It is okay if the small pieces extend slightly beyond the side edges of the bag, as this can be trimmed away after stitching. (figure 13)

8 Once these small pieces are in place, you can add the zipper tabs. To do this, cut two 2½"×6" pieces from Fabric B and fusible interfacing. Fuse the interfacing to the wrong side of the fabric, then stitch these together to create handles following the instructions for handles in Essential Techniques (pages 16–17).

9 Once the zipper tabs have been completed, cut this piece into two 3" lengths. Fold each tab in half to measure 1½" and add to each end of the zipper, centering on the small rectangle added to each end in Step 8. Stitch across the ends, ¼" in from the raw edges. (figure 14)

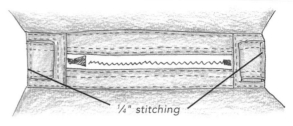

¼" stitching

figure 14

ADDING THE BAG BOTTOM

1 Cut two 9"×19" pieces from Fabric D and one 8"×18" piece from Peltex. Center the Peltex on the wrong side of one of the fabric pieces and fuse. Using temporary adhesive, apply the remaining fabric piece (right-side out) to the other side of the Peltex. There should be a ½" margin of fabric all the way around the Peltex. (figure 15) Stitch ¼" in from the outside edges of the Peltex to hold the pieces together. The fused side will be the one that faces the exterior of the bag; you can mark it with a safety pin to help distinguish the exterior from the interior, if needed.

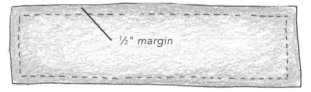

½" margin

figure 15

2 Add the Bag Bottom to the Main Bag pieces with the *lining* sides together. (This may seem backward, but keep going! You'll end up creating a French seam that will conceal this seam.) Stitch together with a ¼" seam. (figure 16) Trim the seam allowance very close to the line of stitching.

3 Turn the bag so that the lining is facing outward. Fold the bag along the bottom seams and press flat. (The right sides of the exterior will be together.)

4 Stitch again along the seam, ⅜" from the edge. This will encase the seam you just stitched and provide a neat French seam inside the bag. (figure 17)

5 Turn the bag right-side out once more and check the seams to be sure they are neat, then press.

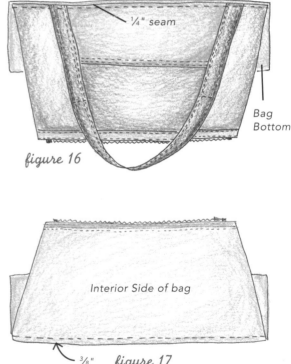

¼" seam

Bag Bottom

figure 16

Interior Side of bag

⅜" *figure 17*

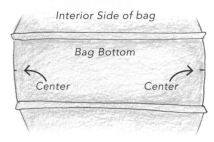

figure 18

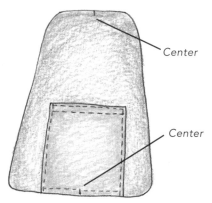

figure 19

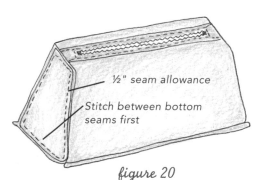

figure 20

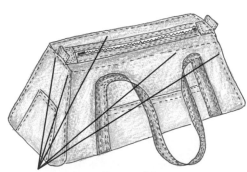

figure 21

ADDING THE BAG ENDS

1   Turn the bag lining-side out once more and mark the center of each end of the Bag Bottom. (figure 18)

2   Clip along the raw edge of the Main Body Bag near the zipper as well as on either side of the center of the bag bottom to ease the curve when the bag ends are added. Be sure that your clips stay well within the ½" seam allowance.

3   Mark the center along the top and bottom of each Bag End piece. (figure 19)

4   Matching the centers, pin the Bag Ends into the openings at each end of the Main Bag pieces with exterior sides together and raw edges even. Ease the fabric together at the corners to fit in the fullness. Make sure that the bag is slightly unzipped so that you can turn the bag right-side out in a later step. *Tip:* You might find it helpful to slightly cut a diagonal off the corner of the bag end to get the two parts to fit together. Keep the ½" seam allowance in mind if you do this—you don't want to completely eliminate your seam allowance here.

5   Stitch across the bottom of the bag first between the bottom seams, and then along the sides and top. (figure 20) *Tip:* I place my hand inside the bag when stitching around the top portion. It helps to guide the fabric as well as prevent puckering.

6   When the stitching is complete, trim the seams down very close to the stitching, watching carefully not to cut into any of the stitching lines.

FINISHING THE BAG

1   Turn the bag right-side out and press, creasing along all seams. Follow the tips in Essential Techniques for getting a professional finish (page 22).

2   To lend more structure to the bag and to conceal the interior seams, fold the bag along one of the side seams and edgestitch between the top and bottom corners. Repeat for the remaining three side seams. You can also press a crease along the top corners near the zipper area, and then add detail stitching. This really does make a difference in the way the finished bag will look. It gives more structure to an otherwise soft bag. (figure 21)

3   Add a zipper charm to the zipper for easy zipping.

creating double-faced quilted fabric

There are some wonderful double-faced pre-quilted fabrics out there, but sometimes you need to create your own. It's relatively quick and easy to do with just a few tools.

materials list

Fabric

Fabric A1—exterior: 1 yard

Fabric A2—lining: 1 yard

Yardage based on 44"-wide cotton fabrics

Additional Tools

1 yard of fusible fleece for quilting

Walking foot attachment (optional)

Spray adhesive

For all other tools, refer to main materials list.

1 Press Fabrics A1 and A2 so that they are smooth.

2 Apply the fusible fleece to the wrong side of Fabric A1.

3 Apply Fabric A2 (right-side out) to the other side of the fleece. It might be helpful to use temporary adhesive spray to hold the fabric/fleece layers together while you quilt.

4 I personally like the diagonal quilting lines, but you can do whatever you like to quilt the two fabrics together. If you would like to do diagonal lines, start at one corner and, using your quilting ruler, draw a line at a 45-degree angle with a chalk pencil. Following this line, create more parallel lines spaced about 2" apart. You can choose to make them closer together or farther apart if you wish.

5 Draw lines at 45 degrees going in the other direction in the same manner. This should create a diamond-shaped pattern on the fabric. (figure 22) If you would rather do horizontal and vertical lines, or even a random meandering pattern, go for it!

6 Quilt together through all thicknesses, starting at the first corner-to-corner lines. I *highly* recommend that you use a walking foot attachment for the quilting lines. It makes the fabrics feed through the machine evenly, preventing small tucks or puckering.

7 Once the fabrics have been quilted together, press the entire piece to smooth it out, then use it just as Fabric A is used to make the bag.

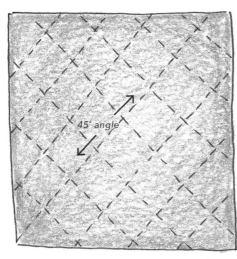

45° angle

figure 22

TULIP TOTE

The Tulip Tote is a medium- to large-size shoulder bag, perfect for everyday use. The exterior is soft-sided, but because of the bag's shape, this one still stands nicely all on its own. This purse just goes to show that interesting elements can come from just about anywhere—the large grommets are from the drapery section. The interior offers pockets on both sides to keep you organized so everything is at your fingertips. Once I had designed this bag, it just looked like a tulip to me with its graceful curvy shape, thus the Tulip Tote!

my initial sketch

Featured in three fabrics and with an option to make a wool and silk version (see pages 70–71), there are a lot of opportunities to make this bag your personal style statement. Look around when shopping for fabrics! This bag would be wonderful made from a textured linen or a lighter-weight home decorating fabric.

    I embellished the bag with a neat decorative pin with a bit of tulle on one side of the bag. Look through your jewelry box and see if there is one that you haven't worn in a long time that might be just that perfect bit of bling your bag is begging for. You can also pick up pretty, decorative pins fairly inexpensively at major department stores.

materials list

Fabric

Fabric A—bag exterior: ½ yard

Fabric B—bag lining & handles: 1 yard

Fabric C—interior pockets & binding: ½ yard

3"×12½" piece one-sided fusible stabilizer (Peltex 71)

½ yard fusible fleece (Thermolam Plus)

1⅔ yards fusible interfacing for light- to mid-weight fabrics

Fabric yardage based on 45"-wide cotton fabrics.

The materials list on page 70 lists yardages for the wool & silk variation with the flower embellishment.

Other Materials

One ¾" magnetic snap

Four 1³⁄₁₆" drapery grommets

Rotary cutter, ruler and mat

Sharp, pointed scissors

Removable marking pencil

Heavy-duty machine needle (such as for denim)

Thread to match fabrics

Finished dimensions of the bag:

10"×13"×3" deep at base, not including the handles

figure 1

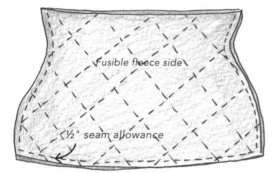

Fusible fleece side

½" seam allowance

figure 2

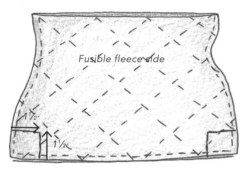

Fusible fleece side

1½"

1½"

figure 3

Quilting Lines

For the quilting lines, I chose to mix it up a bit. When looking at the photos, you will see diagonal lines that are set on a 45-degree angle and spaced 3" apart. I also chose to do some that were double stitched diagonally. If you would like to do the double stitching, stitch on the drawn line, then again ¼" away from the original stitching on each. It's helpful to use a walking foot, but since the fleece is fused to the fabric, it really isn't necessary. Don't rush out and purchase one, but you might want to use it if you have one lying around.

LAYOUT & CUTTING

The Main Bag pattern piece is provided (sheet 2). The ring tabs and handles will be cut following the measurements provided in the instructions using a ruler, rotary cutter and mat.

BAG EXTERIOR

1   This bag has a quilted exterior using the main fabric (Fabric A, or wool in the variation) and fusible fleece. You need to quilt the fabric *before* the pattern pieces are cut. To do this, lay the Main Bag pattern piece onto Fabric A and cut two rectangles slightly larger than the pattern. Cut the same rectangles from fusible fleece. Fuse the fleece onto the wrong side of the fabric. (If you're working with wool, you'll need to spend a little longer with the fusing process so that the heat of the iron properly activates the fleece's adhesive.)

2   Lay the rectangle out on a flat surface with the right side of fabric facing up. With a ruler and removable marking pencil, draw quilting lines on the fabric. (See Quilting Lines sidebar below left.)

3   Once the quilting lines have been stitched on both halves of the exterior (figure 1), press briefly, then place the Main Bag pattern piece onto the fabric and cut out two Main Bag pieces.

If you are adding the flower embellishment, refer to the instructions on page 71.

FORMING SIDE SEAMS AND BOTTOM

1   Place the Main Bag pieces right-sides together with the side and bottom edges even. Stitch together with a ½" seam allowance. (figure 2)

2   Lay the bag out on a flat surface and mark 1½" up from the bottom and side at each corner, including the side seam allowance in the measurement. (figure 3) Cut away the corners and trim down the seam allowances to ¼".

3 At each cut corner, align raw edges and the side and bottom seams right sides together to form the corners of the bag. Stitch across with a ½" seam, then trim the seam allowance to ¼".

4 Clip the curves along the side of the bag, then turn right-side out and press (see page 22 in Essential Techniques).

5 Place the 3"×12½" piece of Peltex inside the bag on the bottom with the fusible side facing the bag. Carefully place your iron inside the bag and fuse the Peltex in place. This reinforces the bottom of the bag and prevents sagging during use.

BAG INTERIOR

1 Using the Main Bag pattern piece once more, cut two each from Fabric B and fusible interfacing. Fuse the interfacing to the wrong side of the fabric.

2 For the interior pockets, cut two rectangles. One will measure 10½" tall × 13½" wide and the other will be 8½" tall × 12½" wide. Cut the same size rectangles from fusible interfacing and fuse to the wrong sides of fabric.

3 Fold each rectangle in half, right sides together, so that its height is reduced by half (5¼" and 4¼" respectively).

4 Stitch the pockets together along the sides and bottom, leaving a 3" opening along the bottom edge for turning. Clip the corners diagonally. (figure 5) Turn right-side out and press. Now edgestitch the top folded edges of each pocket.

5 On the interior bag pieces, mark 4" down from the top on one and 4½" down from the top on the other. Place the smaller pocket's upper edge along the 4" mark (refer to figure 6) and the larger pocket's upper edge on the 4½" mark and pin in place, centered from side to side.

6 Edgestitch the side and bottom edges of each pocket. Mark the smaller pocket 4" in from each end to divide into three equal parts, then stitch down the marked lines. (figure 6)

7 Mark in 5" from each side of the larger pocket to divide it into three sections. (figure 7) Note that the center section will be about 3" wide, so this pocket is not evenly divided. If you wish to divide your pocket differently, please do so. Stitch down the marked lines.

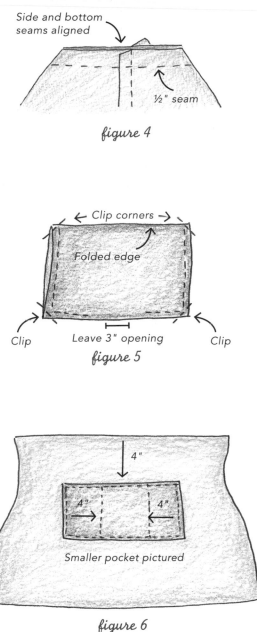

Side and bottom seams aligned

½" seam

figure 4

Clip corners

Folded edge

Clip

Leave 3" opening

Clip

figure 5

4"

4"

4"

Smaller pocket pictured

figure 6

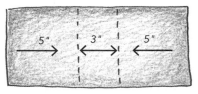

5"

3"

5"

figure 7

Detail for larger pocket

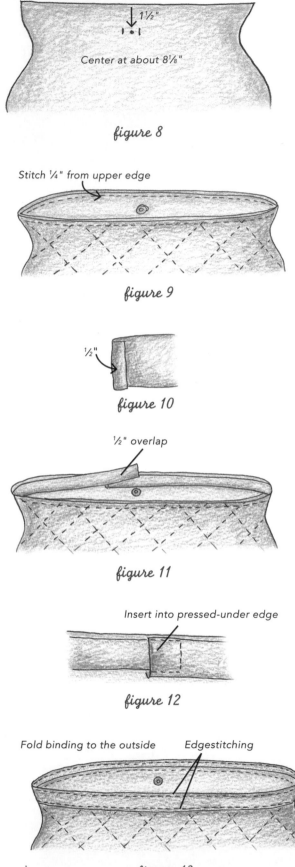

↓ 1½"

Center at about 8⅛"

figure 8

Stitch ¼" from upper edge

figure 9

½"

figure 10

½" overlap

figure 11

Insert into pressed-under edge

figure 12

Fold binding to the outside   Edgestitching

figure 13

8 For the magnetic snap placement, measure 1½" down from the top and mark at the center (about 8⅛" in from the sides) on each interior piece. Mark the prong placement on either side of this mark (figure 8), then snip small openings. Insert the snap, and fold the prongs to the wrong side.

9 Sew the interior together in the same manner as the exterior (Steps 1–5 under Forming Side Seams and Bottom), *except* use a ⅝" seam allowance. This slightly larger seam allowance helps reduce the bulk of the seams and makes the exterior bag and lining pieces fit together nicely.

SEWING THE BAG TOGETHER

1 Place the interior bag inside the exterior with the *wrong* sides together. Match the side seams and upper raw edges. Pin in place, then stitch around the top edge, ¼" in from the raw edges. (figure 9)

2 For the binding, cut a strip from Fabric C 2" × the width of the fabric. Trim off the selvedges, then turn ½" to the wrong side along one of the ends and press. (figure 10)

3 Fold the strip in half lengthwise with wrong sides together and press.

4 Starting with the pressed-under end, place the binding against the top edge of the lining. Pin all the way around until you reach the pressed-under end. Allow for ½" overlap and trim away the excess. (figure 11)

5 Open out the pressed-under end of the binding and place the cut end inside. (figure 12) Finish pinning, then stitch around the top of the bag with a scant ⅜" seam.

6 Fold the binding over to the outside and press. Pin in place, then edgestitch the lower folded edge in place. Edgestitch the top edge of the binding also. (figure 13)

GROMMETS & HANDLES

1   For the grommets, lay the bag out on a flat surface. Place one half of the grommet on top of the bag with the outer edge of the grommet 2½" from the side seam and just below the finished edge of the binding. Use a removable marking pencil to trace the inner circle of the grommet. (figure 14)

2   Use the grommet template that came with the product to trace a slightly larger circle. (figure 15) This will create a perfectly sized circle for installing the grommet. Follow the manufacturer's instructions for snapping the grommet onto the bag. Repeat for the remaining grommets.

3   Cut four strips 2½" × the width of fabric from Fabric B for the handles and nine strips 2½" × the width of the interfacing from fusible interfacing. Fuse the interfacing to the wrong side of the fabric, overlapping by ¼" as necessary. (If you're making the wool variation, test a set of strips with and without the interfacing—you don't want too much bulk in the finished handle, and some wools are thicker than others.)

4   Follow the instructions in Essential Techniques for making the handles (pages 16–17).

5   Once the handles have been made, add one more line of stitching down the center of each to complete five lines of stitching on each one. (figure 16) Trim the handles to 43" in length.

6   Place the end of one of the handles through one grommet opening, going from the exterior toward the interior of the bag. Bring up the end and turn under the raw edge twice by ½" to conceal it. Pin the folded end of the handle in place. (Note: if the handles have been made from wool, complete a tight zigzag stitch along the raw edges of the handles, then turn up only *once* to reduce bulk.)

7   Place the remaining end of that handle through the grommet hole on the same side of the bag, being careful not to twist the handle. Turn the end up as before and pin. Repeat with the remaining handle on the other side of the bag.

8   Try the bag on your shoulder and make any length adjustments to the handles. It may be that you prefer shorter handles. If so, be sure to cut off an equal amount from each handle, then edge- and topstitch in place. (figure 17)

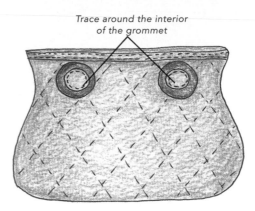

Trace around the interior of the grommet

figure 14

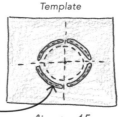

Template

Use outer openings of template to slightly enlarge circle, then cut out

figure 15

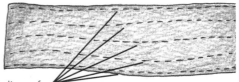

Five lines of stitching on handle

figure 16

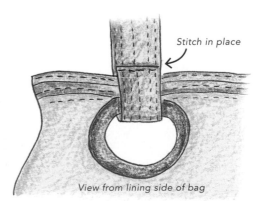

Stitch in place

View from lining side of bag

figure 17

WOOL & SILK VARIATION
with Floral Embellishment

On the wool variation I made, I also created this spectacular floral embellishment. After quilting the exterior fabric (see Steps 1–3 on page 66), follow these steps, and then return to the instructions on page 66, starting with Forming Side Seams and Bottom.

materials list

Fabric

Wool (60" wide medium weight)—bag exterior, handles and flower: ¾" yard

Silk (45" wide)—lining, interior pockets and binding: ¾" yard

Contrasting silk—outer edge of flower: ⅛ yard

Netting (54" wide)—flower detail: ¼ yard

For interfacing, refer to main materials list.

Additional Tools

Ruffler attachment

Hand sewing needle

For all other tools, refer to main materials list.

1. To create a flower for one side of the exterior, cut the following:
   2 strips: 1½" × width of the fabric from wool
   3 strips: 2" × width of the fabric from netting
   1 strip: 3" × width of the fabric from contrasting silk
   After all of the strips have been cut, fold the silk strip in half lengthwise and press.

2. For all strips, add one strip of netting on top. The netting will extend beyond the width of the wool or silk by ½" along one side.

3. Stitch the netting and strips together along the sides where the netting and fabric are aligned. If the netting extends beyond the length of the strip, just trim the excess away.

4. Once all netting has been attached, run the strips through a ruffler attachment set at every stitch. I find it helpful to have the netting side against the feed dogs so that it does not catch on the machine foot during sewing. If you don't have a ruffler attachment, see page 74 to make your own gathered strips.

5. After all of the strips have been ruffled, begin by placing the silk/net ruffle onto the bag with the net-side facing up. Form a circle, approximately 2" from the top edge, 1½" from the bottom and 4" in from the sides. This should form about an 8" circle. (figure 1)

6. Pin in place and stitch on top of strip's previous stitching. With the net-side facing up, start with the first wool strip and place the ruffle just inside the silk one. Begin stitching and continue in a spiral pattern with the rows close together until the strip has been sewn down. (figure 2)

7. Slightly overlap with the next wool strip and continue in this pattern until there is about a 1½" wide circle at the center. Stop stitching. Trim the end of this partially attached strip to create a curved edge (figure 3) and begin rolling it up to form the center of the flower.

8. There may be too much length left, in which case you'll need to trim it down. You want the flower to have a loose appearance, but not *too* loose. Use a hand needle and thread to take a few stitches at the base of the rolled-up portion to keep it from unrolling, then lay the base against the bag and hand-stitch in place. Continue to hand-stitch any of the loose portions of the flower in place. Once the flower is complete, you can continue with the bag construction, beginning on page 66.

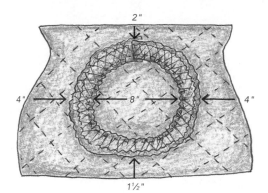

2"
4" 8" 4"
1½"

figure 1

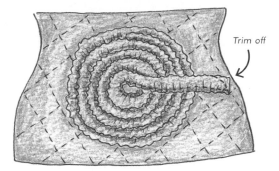

Trim off

figure 2

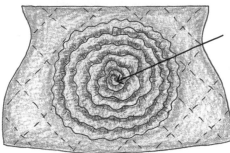

Hand-stitch the rolled-up base in place at center

figure 3

RUFFLE HOBO BAG

The Ruffle Hobo bag is based on one of my bag patterns with Serendipity Studio called the Sylvia Sling. I have always thought that this bag would look terrific with some ruffle "fluff," so I revisited the design and made some changes here and there to make the ruffle idea work with the shape. I love how it came out! The bias strip ruffles give you an opportunity to use some of the great pre-cut fabric strips available in many independent sewing shops. So if you are in love with a lot of different fabrics, this bag is for you!

my initial sketch

This bag would be fabulous with the ruffles made from bias strips out of silk! You could piece several colors of silk together, or just use one solid color. You would need about 1¼" yards of 45"-wide silk for this look from one color, or split that yardage equally depending on how many different colors you would like to piece together. The cutting of the strips and construction would be the same. Another idea—if you don't fancy ruffles—leave them off and have a smooth, tailored bag.

materials list

Fabric

Fabric A—main exterior (underneath ruffles): ⅓ yard

Fabric B—side/bottom of bag: ⅙ yard

Fabric C—exterior zipper panels: ⅛ yard

Fabric D—lining (includes interior zipper panels): ⅝ yard

Fabric E—handles: ⅓ yard, or ⅙ yard *each* of two different fabrics

Fabric F—interior pockets: ⅓ yard

Ruffles and interior seam binding: 1 pre-cut roll of 2½"-wide strips

All fabric yardage is based on 45"-wide cotton fabrics.

Other Materials

Fusible interfacing for light- to mid-weight fabrics: 1⅝ yards

Fusible fleece (Thermolam Plus): ⅓ yard

One-side fusible (Peltex 71): 1 yard

One 14" sport zipper (can be separating or closed bottom)

1½"-wide buckle for handle

Heavy-duty machine needle

Matching polyester thread

Removable marking pen or chalk pencil

Ruffler attachment foot

Rotary cutter, ruler and mat

Sharp, pointed scissors

1 zipper charm

Turning tool

Hand-sewing needle

Temporary spray adhesive

Finished dimensions of the bag:

7" tall × 14" wide × 4" deep, with a 20" handle

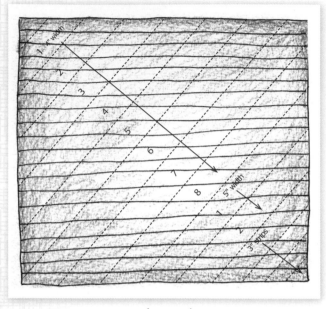

figure 1

Gathering Without a Ruffler Attachment

If you do not own a ruffler attachment, you can complete the gathering of the strip units by completing two rows of gathering stitches, ¼" and ⅜" away from the top raw edges. Leave long tails of thread at the beginning and end of the strip units so that the bobbin threads may be pulled up to gather the fabric.

LAYOUT & CUTTING

The pattern sheets include pieces for the Main Bag Side/Bottom (sheet 1), Interior Pocket (sheet 6), Front Handle (sheet 3), Back Handle (sheet 6) and Main Bag (sheet 5). The Zipper Panels, Ruffle Strips and Bias Binding will be cut from measurements provided in the instructions using a ruler, rotary cutter and mat. Seam allowance for this bag are ½" unless otherwise stated.

CREATING THE BIAS RUFFLES

1 You will create the ruffles from a pieced unit of fabric that you will create by stitching together the pre-cut 2½" fabric strips (each 40½" long). Choose twenty 2½"-wide strips from the pre-cut roll, or cut twenty 2½"-wide by 40½"-long strips from fabrics of your choice. Place them horizontally in a pleasing order. Set aside leftover strips from a pre-cut roll to create binding.

2 Once you have decided on an order for the strips, begin piecing them into one large unit. Place two strips right sides together, and then sew along the length of the strips with a ¼" seam allowance. (I like to use my serger for this.) Continue sewing strips in this manner until all twenty strips are sewn together. This should create a unit that is 40½" × the width of the fabric. Press all of the seams to one side. (figure 1)

3 Following the Cutting on the Bias instructions in Essential Techniques (pages 14–15), begin cutting the strip unit into eight 4"-wide strips. (You will need approximately 8 yards' worth and no more.) Use the leftover portion to cut 1½ to 2 yards' worth of 5" strips (two strips) and three 3" strips for the bias binding (figure 1).

4 Once all strips have been cut, piece all of the 4"-wide strips together, following the instructions in the Essential Techniques. Repeat this process for the 5" strips. Still following the Essential Techniques, trim the ends and fold the strips in half and press, readying them for the ruffler foot.

5 Serge or zigzag stitch the raw edges of the ruffle strip units to prevent fraying before ruffling them, then edgestitch (page 16) along the folded edge.

6 Ruffle both strip units with the ruffler attachment set at every stitch, ¼" in from the raw edge. Do *not* press the ruffles flat after stitching. Set the ruffled strip units aside until the bag exterior has been prepared.

PREPARE THE MAIN BAG

1 Cut out two Main Bag pieces each from Fabric A and from the fusible fleece. Fuse the fleece onto the wrong sides of each Main Bag piece.

2 Using an awl or other sharp object, punch a hole through the pattern at each *circle* marking. Using temporary adhesive spray, place the pattern on the *right* side of one Main Bag piece and transfer *all* pattern markings to the fabric. Peel away the pattern piece and repeat on the other Main Bag piece. (figure 2)

ADDING RUFFLES

1 You will add the 4"-wide and 5"-wide ruffles (now 2"-wide and 2½"-wide, respectively) to the Main Bag. First add the 4"-wide ruffles, beginning at the lower end of the bag. Take the 8-yard-long strip of 4"-wide ruffles and lay its top (gathered) edge carefully along the bottom marked ruffle placement line, with about half of the ruffle extending beyond each raw side edge. Pin in place and cut the ruffle strip. Stitch ruffle to bag over the ruffle's edge stitching. (figure 3) Place, pin and stitch the ruffle strip in the same manner along each ruffle placement line *except the top one*. Repeat on other Main Bag piece.

2 Place and stitch the 5"-wide ruffle strip along the top ruffle placement line in the same manner as you did the 4"-wide ruffles. Repeat on other side of bag. (figure 4)

3 Stitch ¼" in from the curved side edges. It is okay if the ruffles slightly extend beyond the bag edge. Once the stitching is complete, carefully trim away any ruffle extensions. (figure 5)

Pre-Cut Fabric Rolls

If you're using a pre-cut fabric roll for this bag, you'll have leftover strips. Some of these you can use for the interior binding, and others can be set aside for another project.

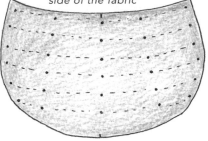

Transfer the pattern markings to the right side of the fabric

figure 2

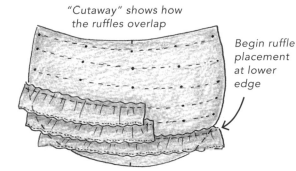

"Cutaway" shows how the ruffles overlap

Begin ruffle placement at lower edge

figure 3

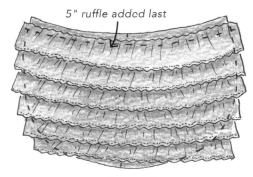

5" ruffle added last

figure 4

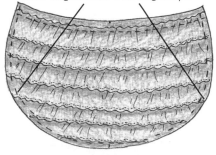

Stitch ¼" in from the edges, then trim ruffle edges even with bag shape

figure 5

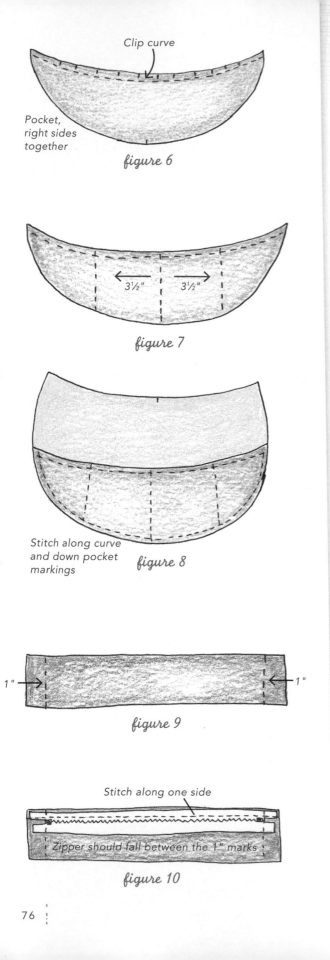

Clip curve

Pocket,
right sides
together

figure 6

3½" 3½"

figure 7

Stitch along curve
and down pocket
markings

figure 8

1" 1"

figure 9

Stitch along one side

Zipper should fall between the 1" marks

figure 10

PREPARE THE LINING & INTERIOR POCKETS

1 Using the Main Bag pattern piece, cut out two lining pieces from Fabric D and two from the fusible interfacing. Transfer the center markings to the Fabric D pieces, then fuse the interfacing to the wrong side of each fabric piece. Using the Interior Pocket pattern piece, also cut four pocket pieces from Fabric F and four from fusible interfacing. Transfer the center markings to the Fabric F pieces, then fuse interfacing to the wrong side of each pocket piece.

2 Place two of the pocket pieces right-sides together and stitch with a ¼" seam allowance along the top edge only. Clip seam allowances (figure 6), then turn so that the pocket pieces are wrong-sides together. Press along the seam at the top edge, then edgestitch. Repeat for the two remaining pocket pieces.

3 Mark down the center of the pocket, then 3½" to either side of center. (figure 7)

4 Pin one pocket to the lining along the bottom edge, matching the center markings. Stitch the pocket to each lining along the outside edges, about ¼" from edge. Then stitch down the markings dividing the pocket into four parts, backstitching at the beginning and end of stitching lines. (figure 8)

PREPARE THE ZIPPER PANEL

1 Cut two 16½" × 2¼" zipper panels each from Fabrics C and D. Fuse interfacing to the wrong side of each zipper panel.

2 Mark in 1" from narrow edges on all four panel pieces. (figure 9)

3 If your sport zipper is the separating type, you will need to secure the ends so they don't separate when using the bag. This is simple to do. Just drop the feed dogs on your machine and set it for a tight zigzag stitch set at the widest setting. With the zipper closed, stitch across the zipper teeth just above the zipper stop. Test the zipper to be sure that the stitches will hold, then proceed to the next step.

4 Center the zipper facedown onto the right side of one of the exterior zipper panels (Fabric C) between markings, with the edge of the zipper tape even with side edge of panel. Use a zipper foot to stitch zipper in place along the one side.

5 Place an interior zipper panel (Fabric D) right-sides together against the strip with the zipper attached. Align markings and panel edges with the zipper sandwiched between the two panels. Stitch the panels together over exterior panel stitching done in Step 4. (figure 11)

6 Press the panels away from the zipper, taking care not to apply too much heat to the zipper teeth. (Pin the Interior and Exterior Zipper Panels together.)

7 Repeat Steps 5–7 for the other side of the Zipper Panel.

ADD THE ZIPPER PANEL TO THE BAG PIECES

1 To add the Zipper Panel to the Main Bag piece, unpin the panel pieces and open one side out so that the exterior Zipper Panel edge is free from the remainder of the Zipper Panel unit. I find it helpful to pin the lining portion of the panel to the other side so that it stays out of the way.

2 Pin one of the Main Bag pieces to the edge of opened-out exterior Zipper Panel pieces, right sides together, with the top edges of the bag just barely extending past the 1" markings on the Zipper Panel at either end and raw edges even. The Zipper Panel will extend beyond the bag piece itself. Stitch together. (figure 12)

3 Repeat this with the lining for that side of the bag, using the interior portion of the Zipper Panel.

4 Repeat this process for the other side of the Main Bag and lining. Open out the pieces away from the Zipper Panel and press all seams toward the panel. Pin the edges of each side (Main Bag and Lining) wrong sides together with center marks and zipper panel seams aligned. Stitch along the outer edges of the Main Bag lining *only* to hold them together. (figure 13)

5 Edgestitch on the Zipper Panel along the seam that joins it to the Main Bag side. Stitch again ¼" away from stitching. Stitch again next to the zipper along the seam, using your zipper foot to get near the teeth. Stitch again ¼" away from edgestitching. (figure 13)

6 Fold along the seam where the Zipper Panel joins the Main Bag, and press to crease it slightly. Repeat for other side.

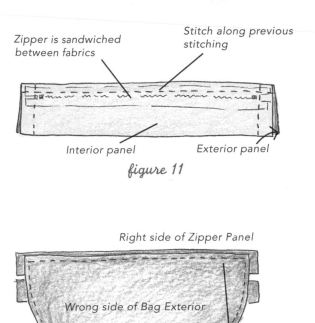

Zipper is sandwiched between fabrics

Stitch along previous stitching

Interior panel

Exterior panel

figure 11

Right side of Zipper Panel

Wrong side of Bag Exterior

figure 12

Stitch together with ½" seam allowance

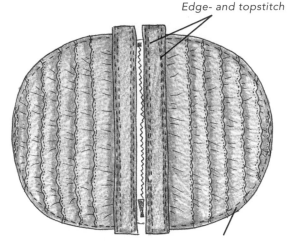

Edge- and topstitch

figure 13

Stitch together (all layers)

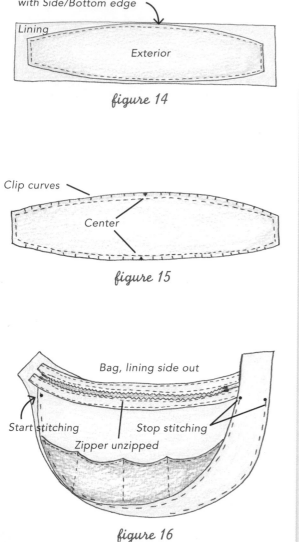

Cut away lining to be even
with Side/Bottom edge

Lining

Exterior

figure 14

Clip curves

Center

figure 15

Bag, lining side out

Start stitching

Stop stitching

Zipper unzipped

figure 16

PREPARE THE SIDE/BOTTOM AND ADD TO BAG

1 Cut one Side/Bottom piece from Peltex and set aside. Cut a strip 5" × the width of fabric from Fabrics B and D for Side/Bottom exterior and lining of the bag.

2 Lay the exterior Fabric B wrong-side facing the fusible side of the Peltex. The ends of the fabric will extend beyond the ends of the Peltex and be a small amount wider as well. This will be trimmed away in the following steps.

3 Fuse the fabric to the Peltex. Flip the piece over and trim away the extra fabric at the ends and sides near each end.

4 Spray the Peltex side of this piece with an adhesive, then, wrong sides together, place the lining piece on top, smoothing the fabric as you apply it to prevent wrinkles or puckering. Transfer all pattern markings to the fabric, making small snips into the fabric for the centers. Keep all markings or snips inside the seam allowances.

5 Flip the piece over and follow the cut edge of the Peltex, stitching through all thicknesses about ¼" from the edges.

6 Trim away the excess fabric of the lining to be even with the other layers. (figure 14) Clip the center of the piece and also clip along both long edges to prepare it for sewing to the bag. (figure 15)

7 Turn the Main Bag (with zipper) so that the lining is facing out, with the zipper open. With the lining side of the Side/Bottom piece facing out, match up the center marks at the bottom, align the raw edges and pin along one long edge of the Side/Bottom piece. The ends of the Side/Bottom will extend beyond the ends of the Zipper Panel. I find it helpful to pin the Zipper Panel portion to the Side/Bottom piece so that it is easier to start and stop the stitching.

8 Stitch the Side/Bottom and Main Bag pieces together along the pinned edge. Start stitching just below the Zipper Panel seam on one end and stopping when you reach this same point on the other end. (figure 16) Trim down the seam to a scant ¼", leaving the entire seam allowance intact above the line of stitching.

9 Repeat this process for the other Main Bag-Side/Bottom seam.

10 To make bias binding strips for the interior seams, cut a series of 2¼" wide strips from the leftover pieced strips for the ruffles. Follow the instructions in Essential Techniques (pages 14–15) to create a binding strip.

11 With the bag inside out, pin the binding strip to the Side/Bottom piece with the raw edges even and the end of the binding about 1" beyond the start of stitching. Pin all the way around, stopping 1" beyond where the line of stitching ends. Cut away any extra.

12 Stitch the binding to the seam, following the seam stitching line. Trim away the extra binding that extends beyond the stitching at each end. (figure 17) Fold the binding over the seam so that the folded edge just covers the stitching and pin in place. Fold the binding over the seam so that it just covers the stitching. Pin in place, and then stitch. Repeat for the remaining seam.

13 Turn the bag right-side out, smoothing out the seam where the Side/Bottom and Main Bag join. Turn out each end of Zipper Panel and Side/Bottom so that they are fully turned to the exterior and raw edges are exposed. These should resemble tubes at each end. (figure 18)

14 Zip the bag closed and turn in the seam allowance on the Side/Bottom piece so that it lies nicely underneath the zipper panel. Pin in place. Measure across the end. It should be about 3" wide (in preparation for the handle). Press each end so that it lies flat.

15 Open the bag once more and use your hand to push out and even up the seams. Take the bag where the Side/Bottom and Main Bag are joined and crease it with your hands. Also press along this seam in this manner to create a crisp, professional finish. Follow the instructions in Essential Techniques (page 22) for additional pressing.

HANDLES

1 Using the Front Handle and Back Handle pattern pieces, cut two pieces each from Fabric E and interfacing. Press under ½" along the wide bottom edge of one of the Front Handle pieces and one of the Back Handle pieces (the ones that will be on the inside of the handle facing the zipper panel).

2 Pin the handle pieces right sides together. Starting and stopping at the pressed/folded edges, stitch along the long edges and angled, narrow ends. Leave the folded edge unstitched. (figure 19)

3 Trim across the stitched ends and cut corners diagonally to reduce bulk. Leave side seam allowances intact. (figure 20)

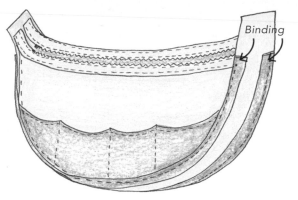

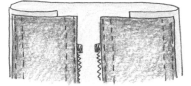

Binding

figure 17

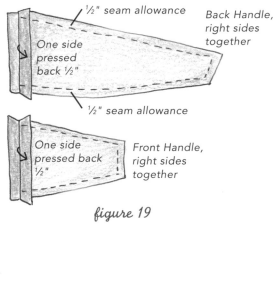

figure 18

½" seam allowance

Back Handle, right sides together

One side pressed back ½"

½" seam allowance

One side pressed back ½"

Front Handle, right sides together

figure 19

Trim corners

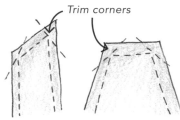

figure 20

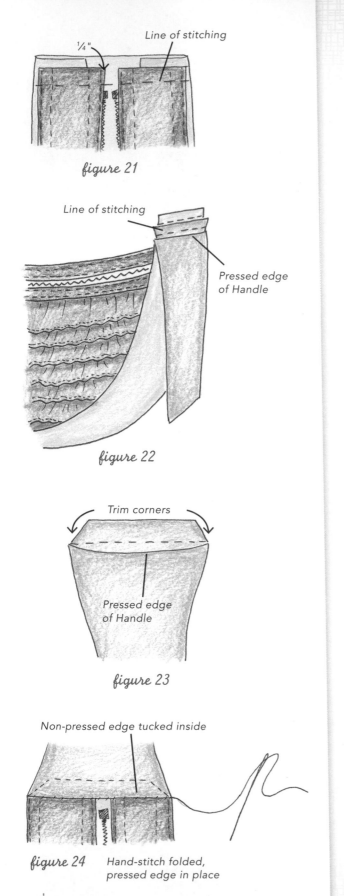

figure 21

Line of stitching

¼"

figure 22

Line of stitching

Pressed edge
of Handle

figure 23

Trim corners

Pressed edge
of Handle

figure 24   Hand-stitch folded,
pressed edge in place

Non-pressed edge tucked inside

4   Turn each handle right-side out and fully turn out corners with a turning tool. (A bamboo skewer or chopstick also works well for this.) Press each handle flat.

5   Stitch across the ends of the bag through all thicknesses, about ¼" down from the raw edge of the zipper panel. (figure 21) Trim away the portion of the Side/Bottom that extends beyond the zipper panel.

6   Join the open end of the Handle (the end with the folded edges) to the Side/Bottom. Pin the right side of the top/outer Handle only to the exterior of the Side/Bottom, leaving the bottom side of the handle (which will face the zipper) free. Align top and side raw edges, and place the pressed fold line of the Handle along the Side/Bottom stitching. Stitch this layer of the Handle to the Side/Bottom just above the fold, being sure to keep the bottom side of the handle free and open. (figure 22)

7   Stitch the handle to the bag just above the pressed edge with the side edges even. Trim down the seam and cut the corners diagonally. (figure 23)

8   Extend the handle outward away from the bag and bring the seam to the inside of the handle opening. Pin so that the folded edge of the handle encases the entire seam and conceals the previous stitching. Stitch close to the folded edge by hand (figure 24), then edgestitch with the machine from the Side/Bottom side of the bag.

9   Edgestitch the Handle edges from the side of the Handle that will be facing out.

10   Repeat for remaining Handle piece.

ADDING A BUCKLE

1 You will need a 1½"-wide buckle with a tongue (I know it sounds weird, but that's what it is called!). The buckle can be round or square.

2 Start by feeding the short end of the Front Handle through the buckle and fold it over the cross bar. Just push the tongue gently to one side to make sure that the buckle will fit onto the handle appropriately.

3 The edge of the handle should fold over about ¾" to the inside. Mark the center of the fold so that you can stitch a small buttonhole as an opening for the tongue.

4 Remove the buckle and make sure that the marking you just made is centered on the handle. Make a small buttonhole, about ¼" long. (figure 25) Carefully cut the buttonhole open, place buckle back onto the handle, place the tongue through the buttonhole and stitch the folded-over edge of the handle in place by hand. (figure 26)

5 Feed the angled end of the Back Handle through the buckle and decide on a finished length for the handle. The one shown is about 20" long from where it attaches to the bag.

6 Mark where you would like to place the second buttonhole on this portion of the handle. Again, check to be sure that the marking is centered, then make the buttonhole. Cut it open and feed it through the buckle, placing the tongue through the buttonhole.

Front Handle piece

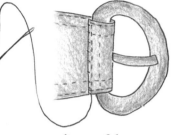

Edge- and topstitching

Buttonhole for buckle tongue

figure 25

Hand-stitch handle end in place

figure 26

VERSATILE
HANDLE HANDBAG

You can use a different fabric to highlight each design feature on this bag—or have the design feature highlight the fabric! There are a lot of great features on this bag. There are elasticized sides that are accented with ruffles, exterior pockets (also accented with ruffles), interior pockets and a magnetic snap closure to keep everything in its place. The loop handle is extra-functional in that it can be pulled through the tabs to be one long handle for wearing over the shoulder or pulled into two smaller handles as a handbag. This bag is fun and casual and would look great from just about any fabric combination.

my initial sketch

Make this handbag your own by adding fun trims or a vintage brooch to one of the outer pockets. It might also be fun to make the entire outer bag from one fabric, then use two other fabrics for the contrast strips and ruffles. Silk would make a gorgeous luxurious addition as a ruffle in this case!

materials list

Fabric

½ yard each of four different fabrics:

Fabric A—main bag center panel fabric, main lining and handle tabs

Fabric B—bag sides and pockets (exterior and interior)

Fabric C—contrast strip for pockets, sides, interior seam binding, handle and top of bag binding

Fabric D—ruffles

All fabric yardage is based on 45"-wide cotton fabrics.

Other Materials

¾ yard Peltex 71 (one-sided fusible stabilizer)

⅓ yard Thermolam Plus fusible fleece

1 yard fusible interfacing for light- to mid-weight fabrics

10" of ¾"-wide elastic

One ¾" magnetic snap

Rotary cutter, ruler and mat

Sharp, pointed scissors

Removable marking pencil

Heavy-duty machine needle (such as for denim)

Thread to match fabrics

Ruffler attachment (optional)

Temporary spray adhesive

Needle-nose pliers

Finished Dimensions

9½" tall × 11" wide at base, 17" wide at opening × 6" deep, not including handle

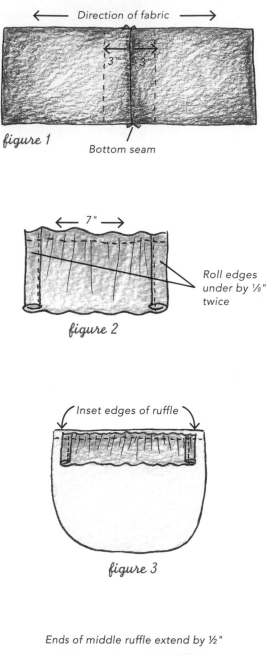

figure 1

Direction of fabric

3" 3"

Bottom seam

figure 2

7"

*Roll edges
under by ⅛"
twice*

figure 3

Inset edges of ruffle

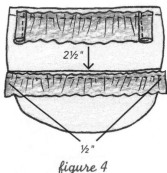

Ends of middle ruffle extend by ½"

2½"

½"

figure 4

LAYOUT

The only pattern piece provided will be for the Exterior Pocket (sheet 3). All other pieces will be cut by measurements given throughout the instructions.

MAIN HANDBAG, LINING & POCKETS

1 From Fabric A, cut four rectangles measuring 13"×10", with the design motif of the fabric parallel to the 13" side. Also cut two rectangles of the same size from the Peltex.

2 For the exterior of the bag, fuse the Peltex to the wrong side of two of the rectangles. Set the remaining two rectangles aside for the lining.

3 Place the two exterior rectangles fabric-sides together and sew along the 10" sides using a ½" seam allowance. This seam forms the bottom of the bag. (If your fabric is directional, make sure the rectangles are turned correctly.) Trim the seam to ¼" and press open. Mark 3" to either side of the bottom seam on the right side of fabric. Repeat for the lining pieces.

4 Using the Exterior Pocket pattern piece, cut four pocket pieces each from Fabric B and interfacing. Apply the interfacing to the wrong side of the fabric for each pocket piece. Set two of the pocket pieces aside as the backing.

5 Cut two strips 2" × the width of the fabric from Fabric D for the pocket ruffle. Trim off the selvedges at each end. Fold the strips in half lengthwise, wrong-sides together, and press.

6 Use a long straight stitch to complete two rows of stitching at ¼" and ⅜" across the raw edges. Pull up the bobbin threads or use a ruffler attachment set at every stitch to gather the strips along the long raw edge, approximately ¼" in from the edge for each strip. Press the ruffled strips flat.

7 Cut two ruffles from one of the strips to be the same length as the top of the pocket, about 7". Turn under the ends of the ruffles by ⅛" twice so that the raw edges are concealed. Edgestitch near the folded edges. (figure 2)

8 Center the ruffles, wrong-side down, along the top edge of two of the pocket pieces (pocket pieces should be right-side up; ruffle will be inset from raw edges of pocket). Sew in place with a ¼" seam. (figure 3)

9 Mark 2½" down from the top of the pocket. Align the raw edge of another piece of the ruffled strip with this mark, with the ends of the ruffle extending beyond the pocket sides by ½". Stitch along the previous stitching on the ruffle to attach. (figure 4) Repeat for other pocket piece. Save the rest of the ruffle strip for the side pockets.

10 Cut two 2"-wide by 8"-long strips from Fabric C for the contrast strip. Fold one strip in half lengthwise with wrong sides together, and press. Lay the contrast strip on top of the lower ruffle with raw edges aligned and with the ends extending beyond the sides by ½". Pin in place and stitch ⅜" from raw edge. (figure 5)

11 Fold the contrast strip upward away from the ruffle and press. Edgestitch the upper folded edge of the contrast strip, then edgestitch the lower edge near the ruffle. Trim away any excess strip/ruffle at pocket sides to be even with the pocket edges. (figure 6) Repeat steps 10 and 11 for other pocket.

12 Place one pocket with ruffle trim against one of the pocket pieces without ruffles, right-sides together, matching the raw edges. Stitch together with a ⅜" seam allowance, taking care not to catch the ruffle strip along the top edge in the side seams. Leave an opening for turning along the bottom of the pocket about 2½" wide. Clip curves and cut corners diagonally (figure 7), then turn right-side out.

13 Press the pocket flat, making sure to fully turn out the corners and curves. Open the top ruffle out away from the pocket. Turn in the edge along the opening by ⅜" and press. Double topstitch the top edge of the pocket below the ruffle. (figure 8)

14 Pin one pocket to each side of the bag exterior (Fabric A) ½" up from the bottom 3" marking and centered from side to side. Double topstitch the pocket edges in place. (figure 9)

15 For the interior pockets, cut two rectangles measuring 10"×8" with the direction of the fabric parallel to the 8" side. Cut two rectangles the same size from interfacing and apply to the wrong side of each piece.

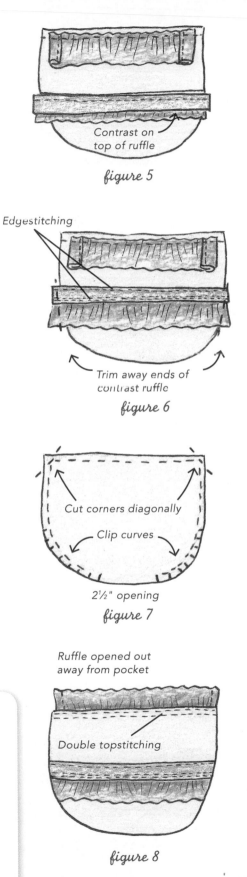

Contrast on top of ruffle

figure 5

Edgestitching

Trim away ends of contrast ruffle

figure 6

Cut corners diagonally

Clip curves

2½" opening

figure 7

Ruffle opened out away from pocket

Double topstitching

figure 8

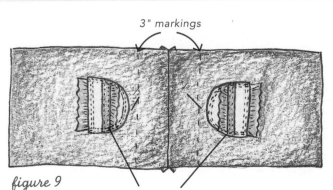

3" markings

figure 9

Double Topstitching

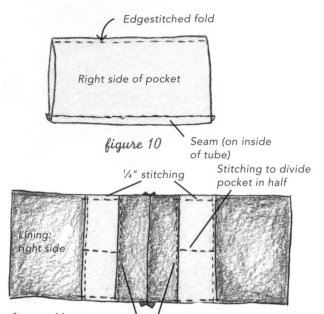

Edgestitched fold

Right side of pocket

figure 10

Seam (on inside of tube)

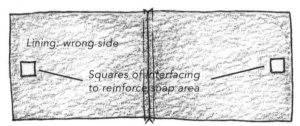

¼" stitching

Stitching to divide pocket in half

Lining: right side

figure 11 Bottom of pocket on 3" marks

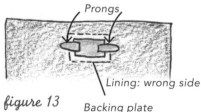

Lining: wrong side

Squares of interfacing to reinforce snap area

figure 12

Prongs

Lining: wrong side

figure 13

Backing plate of snap

¼" stitching

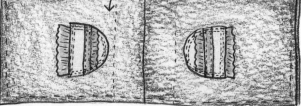

figure 14   Bag and Lining sewn together right sides facing outward

16 Fold the inside pocket pieces in half right sides together so that they measure 10"×4". Stitch along the 10" edge with a ¼" seam allowance, forming a tube. Turn right-side out and press with the seam along one edge. Edgestitch along the pressed folded edge. (figure 10)

17 Sew the two remaining 10"×13" rectangles cut from Fabric A in Step 1 (for the lining) right-sides together with a ½" seam along one of the 10" sides. Trim the seam and press open. Apply the interior pockets to the lining on the right side of fabric with the raw edges along the sides even, and with the seam edge of the pockets along the 3" marking on either side of the bottom seam. Stitch ¼" in from the side edges to attach the pockets (figure 11) and edgestitch along the bottom edge of each pocket. Draw a line down the middle of each pocket at 5" and stitch along the line to divide the pockets in half.

18 On the wrong side of the lining, mark the center at each top edge, then 1¼" down. Cut two small squares of scrap interfacing and apply on top of interfacing already fused to the lining. (figure 12) This will reinforce the area where you will place the magnetic snap.

19 On the right side of the lining, mark the center and then 1¼" down from the top edge for the snap placement. Snip small openings for the snap prongs on either side of the center marking, then place the prongs through the fabric to the wrong side. Slide the backing plate on and bend the prongs outward toward the sides of the bag with needle-nose pliers. (figure 13) Repeat for other half of snap at opposite end of lining.

20 Lay the Lining right-side up on top of the Peltex-exposed side of the Main Bag piece. Align the bottom seams and raw edges. Pin together at bottom seam, then use temporary spray adhesive to attach the lining to the Peltex. This helps to prevent puckers when the layers are stitched together. Stitch in ¼" around entire outer edge and set Main Bag aside. (figure 14)

HANDBAG SIDES, HANDLE & BINDING

1 For the handbag sides, cut four 10" squares from Fabric B. Also cut two 10" squares from fusible fleece. Fuse the pieces to two of the fabric squares. Mark these pieces with a small dot in one corner; this will identify the side that forms the exterior of the bag. Attach the other two squares to the non-fusible side of the fleece with temporary adhesive spray, then stitch in ¼" from all four outside edges.

2 On the exterior side, mark 3½" down from the top edge. Align the raw edge of the ruffle strip to this marking and sew through all thicknesses on top of the previous stitching. (figure 15)

3 Cut a 3"×10" strip from Fabric C, fold in half lengthwise with wrong sides together and press. Add this strip to the ruffle (like you did for the pockets on page 85) and stitch in place. (figure 16) Fold the strip upward away from the ruffle and press. Pin in place and edgestitch both the folded edge and the one near the ruffle. (figure 17) Repeat for other side.

4 Cut two pieces of ¾" wide elastic, 5" long. Insert into the contrast strip casing and stitch across the ends with the edges of elastic and bag even. Clip the center of the bag side along the bottom edge by folding in half and snipping off the corner slightly. (figure 18)

5 Use a long straight machine stitch to complete two rows of stitching along the bottom edge of the Bag Sides at ¼" and ⅜".

6 Clip along the bottom edges of the main bag (Fabric A) piece, starting about 2" before the bottom markings at 3", across the bottom and up the other side to prepare for adding the side pieces. (figure 19)

7 With the lining side facing out for all pieces, pin the Bag Side to the Main Bag. Match the Main Bag's bottom seam with the center marking on the Bag Sides. Match the bottom corners of the Bag Side to the 3" markings on the Main Bag. The top edges of all pieces should be even. Pull the gathering threads along the Bag Sides until it matches in size with the main bag; pin in place.

8 Stitch the Main Bag and Bag Sides together with a ½" seam allowance. (figure 20) Trim the seam down to ¼".

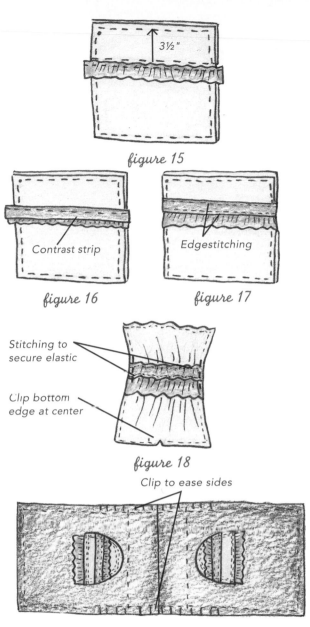

figure 15

Contrast strip

figure 16

Edgestitching

figure 17

Stitching to secure elastic

Clip bottom edge at center

figure 18

Clip to ease sides

figure 19

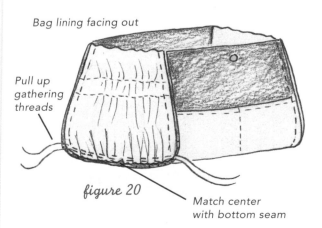

Bag lining facing out

Pull up gathering threads

figure 20

Match center with bottom seam

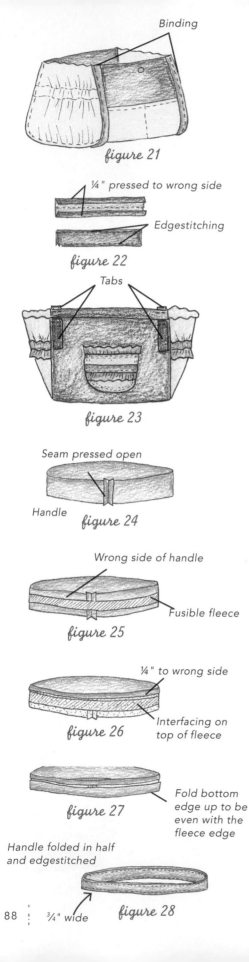

Binding

figure 21

¼" pressed to wrong side

Edgestitching

figure 22

Tabs

figure 23

Seam pressed open

Handle

figure 24

Wrong side of handle

Fusible fleece

figure 25

¼" to wrong side

Interfacing on top of fleece

figure 26

Fold bottom edge up to be even with the fleece edge

figure 27

Handle folded in half and edgestitched

¾" wide

figure 28

9   Cut two strips 2¼"-wide × the width of fabric from Fabric C. Fold in half lengthwise with wrong sides together and press. Add the binding strip to the seam along the Main Bag's interior. Stitch along the previous line of stitching. (figure 21)

10   Fold the binding over the seam to conceal it and pin in place. (figure 21) Edgestitch the folded edge in place. Briefly press the bag while wrong-side out to soften the Peltex, then turn the bag right-side out. Fully turn out the bottom. Fold along the seam lines and press. Continue to press until the bag has a crisp, professional finish. (See Essential Techniques page 22.)

11   Cut four 2"×5" pieces from Fabric A for the handle tabs. Cut four pieces the same size from interfacing and apply to the wrong side of each tab. Fold and press ¼" to the wrong side of each tab along the 5" sides. Fold in half lengthwise wrong-sides together and edgestitch the pressed edges in place; edgestitch the folded side. (figure 22)

13   Add the tabs on top of the main bag portion of the handbag where the side of the bag is joined. Pin in place, then stitch across ¼" from the edge. (figure 23) Set the bag aside.

14   For the handle, cut a 4½"×35" strip from Fabric C. Fold the strip in half crosswise, right-sides together matching raw edges, and sew with a ¼" seam to form a loop. Press the seam open. (figure 24) Cut a piece of fusible fleece 1½"×35". Center the fleece on the wrong side of the handle and press in place. (figure 25)

16   Cut two strips of interfacing, 4½"×20". Add to the wrong side of the handle loop on top of the fusible fleece. Use the second interfacing strip to continue covering the wrong side of the handle, overlapping the interfacing by ¼" when piecing. When the beginning edge of the interfacing is reached, overlap again by ¼" and cut away the excess. (figure 26)

17   Fold one of the handle's raw edges over to the wrong side by ¼" and press. (figure 26) Fold the remaining edge to the wrong side using the edge of the fusible fleece as a guide and press in place. (figure 27)

18   Sew the handle together, fold it in half lengthwise with wrong sides together; match the pressed folded-under edges. It's fine if this causes one edge of the fleece to fold over slightly as well. Edgestitch the two pressed edges together. Fold in half lengthwise once more and edgestitch again, following the previous stitching. This will result in a handle that is a continuous loop approximately ¾" wide. (figure 28)

19 Place the handle around the top edge of the bag over the open tabs. Fold the tabs in half and bring the unsewn end up to be even with the top edge of the bag, encasing the handle. Do this for each tab. Stitch across the tab to hold the handle in place. (figure 29)

20 Cut a 3" strip by width of fabric from Fabric C for the exterior binding at the top of the bag. Trim away the selvedges and press one of the narrow ends to the wrong side by ½". Fold the strip in half lengthwise wrong sides together and press.

21 Starting with the pressed-under edge, pin the binding in place around the entire top edge on the lining side until the pressed-under edge is reached. Overlap the binding by about 1" and cut away excess. Stitch around the top edge about ½" from the top of the bag using a ⅜" seam allowance. (figure 30)

22 Open out the binding away from the bag and press. Fold it over to the outside and press once more. Edgestitch the lower pressed edge, then edgestitch the upper finished edge of the binding. (figure 31)

Enclose handle by folding tabs and stitching

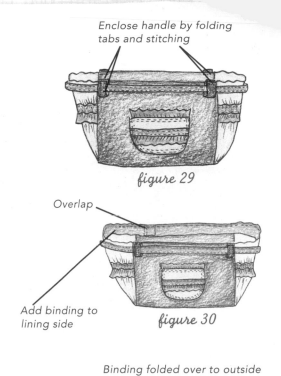

figure 29

Overlap

Add binding to lining side

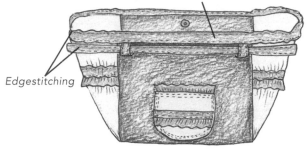

figure 30

Binding folded over to outside

Edgestitching

figure 31

Truly Versatile

The tabs and strap on this bag are designed for versatility. This bag can be held a number of ways. There are two options for a handbag-style hold: the one to the right and the one shown on page 82. Or, you can pull the handle through to create a shoulder bag (left). As a handbag or a shoulder bag, it's just perfect.

SOCIALITE HANDBAG

You'll feel just like a debutante carrying this little beauty! With its lovely curved shape and smooth elegant features, it is most definitely a show-stopper. The Socialite Handbag is a simple yet sophisticated design with a wide base that tapers to a narrow opening. Gently ruched pockets grace the exterior back with the embellished magnetic tab closure completing the design at the exterior front. Divided pockets on one side of the interior help keep your things organized. This bag offers the option of a handbag or shoulder-length handle.

my initial sketch

Make this bag your own by making it from only two fabrics, or even one. A pretty cotton sateen would be a lovely choice for this bag. Of course, the fabric choice will completely change the look of the bag and a nice geometric black and white print would be striking.

materials list

Fabric

Fabric A—bag exterior, exterior pockets and handle: 1 yard

Fabric B—lining and interior pockets: ⅝ yard

Fabric C—interior seam binding, flap, exterior pocket trim and top edge binding: ½ yard

All fabric yardage is based on 45"-wide cotton fabrics.

Other Materials

1 yard Peltex 71 (one-sided fusible stabilizer)

1¼ yards fusible interfacing for light- to mid-weight fabrics

One ¾" magnetic snap

Needle-nose pliers

Rotary cutter, ruler and mat

Sharp, pointed scissors

Removable marking pencil

Heavy-duty machine needle (such as for denim)

Thread to match fabrics

1 large decorative button, brooch or pin for flap embellishment

Temporary adhesive spray

Finished Dimensions

*7½"×16" wide at base, 10" wide at opening x 3" deep
The handle has either a 9" or 12½" drop.*

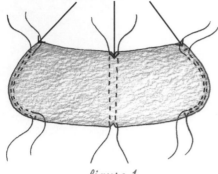

Gathering Stitches

figure 1

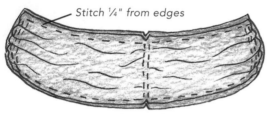

Press gathers flat

figure 2

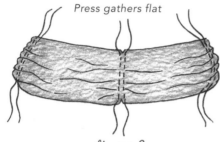

Stitch ¼" from edges

figure 3

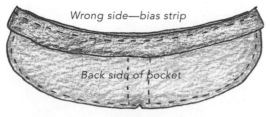

4"

Wrong side

1"

Edgestitching

figure 4

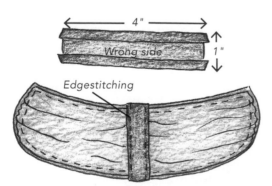

Wrong side—bias strip

Back side of pocket

figure 5

LAYOUT & CUTTING

With the exception of the Main Bag Side, all pattern pieces are provided for this bag: Flap/Closure (sheet 2); Main Bag (sheet 5); and Exterior Pocket Lining/Interior Pocket, Handle and Exterior Ruched Pocket (sheet 6). This will be cut as a strip using a rotary cutter, ruler and mat. Watch the pattern of the fabric closely; fussy cut as desired.

EXTERIOR, LINING & POCKETS

1 From Fabric A: cut two Main Bag pieces, two Handles and one Exterior Ruched Pocket. Cut one Exterior Pocket Lining from Fabric B. Transfer all pattern markings to fabric. From interfacing, cut two Handles and two Exterior Pockets; from Peltex, cut two Main Bags.

2 Apply interfacing to the wrong side of each Exterior Pocket piece (ruched and lining).

3 Sew gathering stitches on the Exterior Ruched Pocket piece (Fabric A). Use the longest straight machine stitch and sew along the outer edge between the notches and down the center from marking. (figure 1)

4 Pull up the gathering stitches until the Exterior Ruched Pocket piece is the same size as the Exterior Pocket Lining (Fabric B) piece and press the gathers flat, arranging the pleats as desired during the ironing process. (figure 2)

5 Pin the two pocket pieces wrong sides together and stitch ¼" in along the edges. (figure 3)

6 From Fabric C, cut a bias strip of fabric, 2" wide by 25" long. See the Essential Techniques (pages 14–15) section for cutting fabric on the bias. From the bias strip, cut one piece 4" long. Fold in ½" along each 4" side to the wrong side and press to get a 1"×4" strip. Place this strip down the center of the pocket (wrong side of strip to right side of fabric), covering the stitches. Pin and edgestitch (page 17) the strip in place. (figure 4)

7 Using the remaining bias strip, pin it right-sides together to the lining side of the pocket along the top edge, with the strip extending slightly at each pocket side. Trim away any excess strip. Sew with a ½" seam allowance. (figure 5)

8 Open out the strip away from the pocket and press. Fold it over the top edge of the pocket and press again, then turn under the lower raw edge to the exterior side about ¼" and press. Edgestitch the lower edge then the upper edge in place. (figure 6)

9 Pin the pocket to the right side of one of the exterior Main Bag pieces, matching up the sides and bottom edge. Stitch together ¼" from the outer edges. Stitch the center of the pocket through all layers, following the previous stitching on the contrast band, pivoting just below the top binding and stitching down the other side to divide the pocket. (figure 7)

10 Cut out two Interior Pockets from Fabric B. Apply interfacing to the wrong side of each Interior Pocket piece. Sew the pocket pieces right-sides together along the top edge, then clip the curve. (figure 8) Turn the pieces right-side out, folding along the seam line and press, with all remaining raw edges even. Pin together, then stitch ¼" in from all raw edges and edgestitch the top along the seam. (figure 9)

11 Find the center of the Interior Pocket. Using a removable marking pencil, mark a vertical line down the center. Then divide those two sides in half, creating marks that will divide this pocket into fourths. Pin the pocket to the right side of one of the Lining pieces, matching up the sides and bottom edge. Stitch ¼" in around the sides and bottom edge, then stitch down the three marks that divide the pocket. (figure 10)

12 Add the large "receiving" side of the magnetic snap to the Exterior Main Bag piece that does not have the Ruched Pocket. To do this, find the center marking, then mark 1¾" below the center for the snap placement. Place the prongs of the snap on either side of the mark and mark for the prongs. Snip at these marks. (figure 11) Insert the snap, then place the plate on the back side. Bend the prongs to the wrong side to secure the snap using needle-nose pliers. (figure 12)

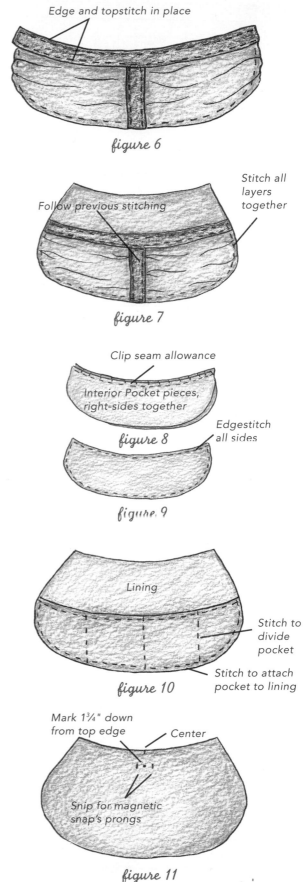

Edge and topstitch in place

figure 6

Follow previous stitching

Stitch all layers together

figure 7

Clip seam allowance

Interior Pocket pieces, right-sides together

figure 8

Edgestitch all sides

figure 9

Lining

Stitch to divide pocket

Stitch to attach pocket to lining

figure 10

Mark 1¾" down from top edge

Center

Snip for magnetic snap's prongs

figure 11

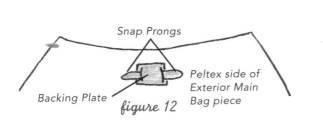

Snap Prongs

Backing Plate

Peltex side of Exterior Main Bag piece

figure 12

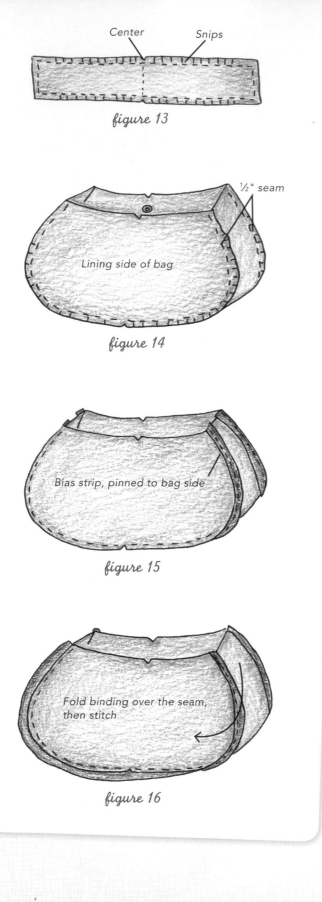

Center   Snips

figure 13

½" seam

Lining side of bag

figure 14

Bias strip, pinned to bag side

figure 15

Fold binding over the seam, then stitch

figure 16

13 Attach the Lining pieces, right-sides facing out, to the Peltex side of the Main Bag pieces with temporary spray adhesive. Be sure to place the Interior Pocket on the *non-pocketed* Main Bag piece. Stitch these together, ¼" in from all edges and set aside.

14 Cut a strip from Peltex measuring 4"×34½". Cut the same size strip from both Fabrics A and B. Place the wrong side of the Fabric A strip against the fusible side of the Peltex and press. Then add the Fabric B piece (right-side up) to the Peltex side using temporary spray adhesive spray. Stitch in ¼" from all outer edges. This is the bottom/side piece.

15 Fold the strip in half and clip at the top and bottom of the fold to mark the center. Complete a series of ⅜" snips along each side of the strip (figure 13) and along the side and bottom of both Main Bag pieces. This will help ease the pieces together when stitching.

16 Pin the right sides of the Main Bag and Bottom/Side pieces together with the Lining facing outward. Begin at the bottom center of the bag, matching markings and work around the curves, making additional snips as necessary to ease the pieces together. Stitch together with a ½" seam. (figure 14)

17 Trim the seam to a scant ¼". Cut several 2½" bias strips from Fabric C and piece together with a ¼" seam, pressing seams open. (See Essential Techniques, pages 14–15.) Two 1-yard pieces should be enough for the interior seam binding. Cut the ends of the strips straight and then fold them in half lengthwise with wrong-sides together and press.

18 Pin each strip to the bag, with raw edges even with the seam's raw edges, and the folded edge in toward the Sides/Bottom piece. The strip must extend at least ⅜" past the top edges of the bag. Stitch, following the bag's seam line.

19 Open out the binding and fold it over the seam edges. (figure 16) Pin in place and edgestitch the outer folded edge in place.

20 Briefly iron the bag to soften the Peltex, then turn right-side out. For a crisp finish, fold the bag at the seams and press. (See Essential Techniques, page 22.)

HANDLES, CLOSURE & BINDING

1 Apply interfacing to the wrong side of both Handle pieces. Sew the Handle pieces right sides together along both long edges with a ½" seam allowance. Clip the curves and leave the entire seam allowance in place. (figure 17) Turn right-side out and press.

2 Double topstitch the finished edges of the handle. See the Essential Techniques section for more detail about double topstitching (page 17).

3 Place the handle on the *inside* of the bag, with the raw edges of the handle against the Bottom/Side piece's top edges. The handle should just fit between the two interior bound seams. Stitch across the handle ends (over the binding) at ⅜" a few times to reinforce. (figure 18)

4 Cut two Flap/Closures from Fabric C and two from interfacing. Apply interfacing to the wrong side of each Flap/Closure piece. To apply the remaining half of the magnetic snap to the Flap/Closure, mark 1¼" up from the center of the rounded edge. Center the snap's prongs on either side of the marking and make marks for the prongs. Snip at the markings. (figure 19) Slip the prongs through the snips and fit the backing plate into place. Fold the prongs over with needle-nose pliers to the wrong side. (figure 20)

5 Sew the Flap/Closure pieces right sides together along the sides and bottom curved edge with a ⅜" seam allowance, leaving the straight end open.

6 Clip the curves along the rounded corners and turn the Flap/Closure tab right-side out. Press. Trim the Peltex piece for the Flap/Closure down by ½" on all sides. Insert it into the open end of the Flap/Closure with the fusible side facing the side *without* the snap. Trim as needed so the Peltex piece fits, completely, yet snugly inside the tab. Iron in place. (figure 21)

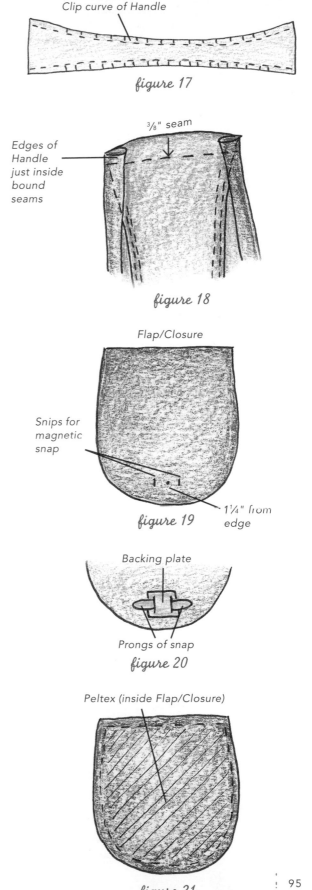

Clip curve of Handle

figure 17

⅜" seam

Edges of Handle just inside bound seams

figure 18

Flap/Closure

Snips for magnetic snap

1¼" from edge

figure 19

Backing plate

Prongs of snap

figure 20

Peltex (inside Flap/Closure)

figure 21

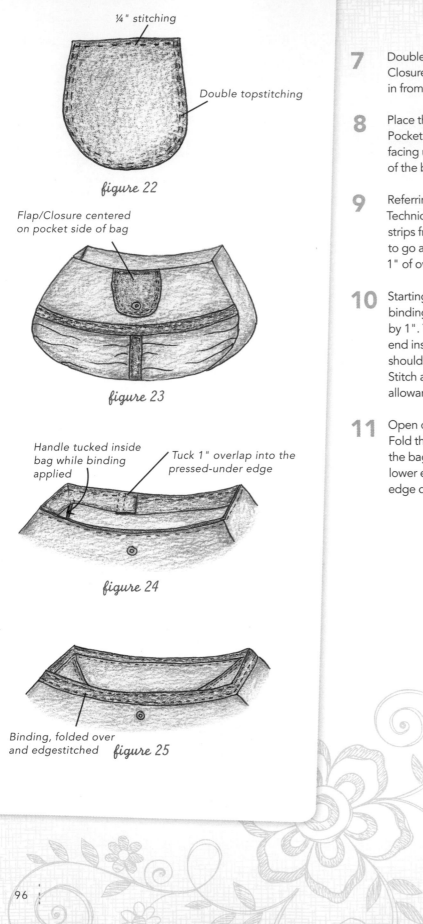

¼" stitching

Double topstitching

figure 22

Flap/Closure centered
on pocket side of bag

figure 23

Handle tucked inside
bag while binding
applied

Tuck 1" overlap into the
pressed-under edge

figure 24

Binding, folded over
and edgestitched   figure 25

7 Double topstitch the finished edges of the Flap/
Closure with the non-snap side facing up. Stitch ¼"
in from raw edges along straight edge. (figure 22)

8 Place the Flap/Closure on the Exterior Ruched
Pocket side of the bag, centered, with the snap side
facing up. Stitch across ⅜" from raw edge at the top
of the bag. (figure 23)

9 Referring to pages 14–15 in the Essential
Techniques section, cut a series of 3½"-wide bias
strips from Fabric C. Piece enough strips together
to go around the top of the bag, with an additional
1" of overlap.

10 Starting with the pressed-under edge, pin the
binding along the lining of the bag, overlapping
by 1". Trim away any excess, and tuck the cut
end inside the pressed-under edge. The handle
should still be resting inside the bag at this point.
Stitch around the top of the bag using a ⅜" seam
allowance. (figure 24)

11 Open out the binding away from the bag and press.
Fold the binding over the seam to the exterior of
the bag and press. Pin in place and edgestitch the
lower edge. Then edgestitch the upper finished
edge of the binding. (figure 25)

12 Bring handle to the outside of the bag and press where the handle joins the bag. With the handle opened out, stitch again along the top edge of the binding, following the previous stitching. This will hold the handle to the outside of the bag during use. (figure 26)

13 Fold the Flap/Closure up away from the bag and press. Edgestitch through all thicknesses along the bottom of the Flap, then again about ½" away from the edgestitching. Fold the Flap around and close at the front of the bag with the other half of the snap. (figure 27)

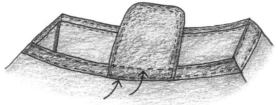

figure 26

Edgestitch through all thicknesses, then again ½" away

figure 27

Ruched Pockets

The subtle texture of the ruched pockets adds a stylish touch.

CHALLENGING BAGS

Up for a real challenge? These bags have everything that an experienced bag-maker loves—lots of construction detail everywhere you look. While no step is difficult, these bags do require a bigger commitment of time and effort, but the end result is worth it.

First up is the Convertible Backpack. I wanted to create a backpack that could also be carried as a bag, depending on your mood. The adjustable straps do just that! The Multi-Tasker Bag is next; it's just perfect for toting around books, crafts, baby stuff, you name it! With a nice zipper closure, it can be easily laid on its side without the worry of losing any contents. The biggest challenge of all is the Laptop Messenger because it's a bag within a bag.

These were my favorite bags to design. I always have a great feeling of accomplishment after completing designs like these. I hope you'll feel that same sense of accomplishment when you make one. You'll certainly earn your bragging rights!

CONVERTIBLE BACKPACK

The Convertible Backpack is a cool, casual look suited to everyday use or travel. The exterior media pocket (also featured on the Laptop Messenger Bag) gives you a convenient place to keep your cell phone and other media devices handy. The interior has a roomy pocket with a zippered closure, perfect for keeping smaller items at hand. The main bag closes with a drawstring and the exterior flap features a metal twist latch. The handles, though, are what really set this backpack apart from the pack—they can convert from shoulder handles to backpack handles with the quick slide of two adjustable rings.

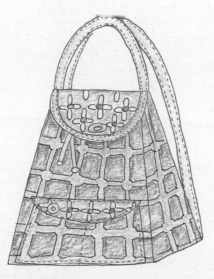

my initial sketch

Feel free to add a different type of latch or add a cord stop to the drawstring. Use a decorative cording for the drawstring instead of making the covered cording. Use home decorating fabrics for the exterior, or make your own exterior fabric from your favorite fabric scraps to create a bag with a Bohemian, patchwork flair.

materials list

Fabric

Fabric A—exterior bag, lining, drawstring covering and exterior media pocket

> *Small:* 1¼ yard; *Large:* 1½ yards

Fabric B—handles, flap binding and bag binding: ⅜ yard (both sizes)

Fabric C—pocket flap, main bag flap and interior pocket: ⅜ yard (both sizes)

All yardage based on 45"-wide cotton fabrics.

Other Materials

Peltex 71 (one-sided fusible stabilizer)

> *Small:* ⅞ yard; *Large:* 1⅛ yards

Fusible interfacing for light- to mid-weight fabrics

> *Small:* 2 yards; *Large:* 2¼ yards

Zipper (*not* sport weight)

> *Small:* 7" ; *Large:* 9"

One 1"×1⅜" metal twist latch

Rotary cutter, ruler and mat

Sharp, pointed scissors

Removable marking pencil

Thread to match fabrics

Heavy-duty machine needle (such as for denim)

1½ yards of ³⁄₁₆" cotton cording for drawstring

One zipper charm

Two 1¼" two-loop sliders for handle adjustment

Three 1¼" D-rings for handles

Twelve ⅜" metal grommets

Temporary spray adhesive

1" strip of hook and loop tape

Finished Dimensions

Small: 12" tall × 10" wide at the base, 7" at the opening and 4" deep. Handles have a 9" drop.

Large (shown at left): 14" tall × 11" wide at the base, 9" at the opening and 5" deep. Handles have a 9" drop.

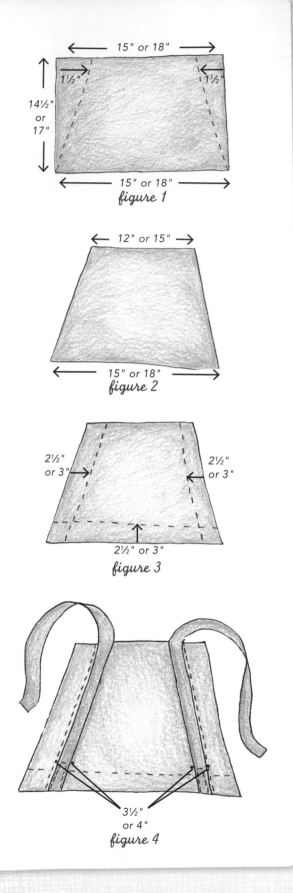

figure 1

figure 2

figure 3

figure 4

2½"
or 3"

2½"
or 3"

2½"
or 3"

3½"
or 4"

15" or 18"

1½"

1½"

14½"
or
17"

15" or 18"

12" or 15"

15" or 18"

LAYOUT & CUTTING

The only pattern pieces provided for this bag are the Media Pocket Flap (sheet 1, sheet 5) and the Bag Flap (sheet 3). The rest of the pieces are cut by measurements given in the instructions using a rotary cutter, ruler and mat.

BAG EXTERIOR, HANDLES & MEDIA POCKET

1 Cut two rectangles from Peltex.
Small: 14½" × 15"
Large: 17" × 18"

2 Lay the Peltex pieces out on a flat surface with the longer side running top and bottom. Measure in 1½" from the two top corners and mark. Using a ruler, align the marking at the top with the bottom corner along one side and draw a diagonal line. Repeat for the other side. (figure 1) Cut on drawn lines to form a trapezoid. The top of the bag piece should now measure: *small*—12" (top), 15" (bottom); *large*—15" (top), 18" (bottom). The height will be 14½" or 17" as originally cut. Repeat for the remaining piece of Peltex. (figure 2)

3 For the exterior bag, cut two rectangles from Fabric A per Step 1. The direction of the design motif should run parallel to the shorter side (14½" or 17"). Fussy cut as needed. Lay the fabric rectangles right-side up on the fusible side of the Peltex, with the 12" or 15" (narrower) width at the top. Fuse together, then trim away the excess fabric on the sides so that all edges are even. On the fabric side, mark in from sides and bottom of each piece on the fabric side with a removable marking pencil: 2½" for *small* and 3" for *large*. (figure 3).

4 Cut four strips 2¼" × the width of fabric from Fabric B. Cut nine 2¼" wide strips from interfacing. Apply the interfacing strips to the wrong side of the fabric strips, overlapping by ¼" as necessary. Make the handle according to the Essential Techniques (pages 16-17). When complete, cut one 4" long piece from each handle for the handle tab.

5 Place handles onto one of the exterior bag pieces (it will be the back of the bag) with the outside edge of handles just inside the 2½" (for *small*) or 3" (for *large*) markings, and bottom edges even. Pin, then mark 3½" (for *small*) or 4" (for *large*) up from bottom edge on either side of handles. This is the pivot point when you stitch the handles down. (figure 4)

6 To attach handles, begin at the lower edge of bag and stitch over the handle edgestitching up to the 3½" (for *small*) or 4" (for *large*) marking. Pivot, backstitch across the handle, pivot, then stitch down the other edge, over handle edgestitching, to the bag bottom. The remainder of the handles remain free. (figure 4)

7 Place one handle tab through *one* D-ring and fold in half. Sew across the end with a ¼" seam allowance. Trim the corners diagonally and position the seam at the center of the back side of the tab. Place the other tab through *two* D-rings, then fold in half and sew together like the first one. (figure 5) The two rings help the handles to lie next to one another as they are pulled through.

8 On the exterior bag back (with handles), place the tab with one D-ring on the left side and the one with two D-rings on the right, inside the 2½" (for *small*) or 3" (for *large*) markings at an angle with lower outer corner ¾" inside the marking and the upper outer corner 1" inside the marking and 1½" down from the top edge. Sew across the lower edge of the tab, pivot turn and stitch up the side to just below the ring. Pivot again and stitch just below the ring, taking care not to break the needle by stitching too closely. Pivot once more and backstitch to where you started stitching. Leave the handles free from these rings at this point; they will be fed through the rings in a later step. (figure 6)

9 For the media pocket, cut one piece from Fabric A and one from interfacing: *small*—8¾" wide × 9" tall; *large*—10½" square. Fussy cut as needed. Apply the interfacing to the wrong side of the fabric.

10 Fold the pocket in half right-sides together and stitch along the sides and bottom with a ¼" seam allow-ance, leaving a 3" opening along the bottom edge. Clip the corners diagonally. Turn the pocket right-side out. (figure 7) Press, turning the opening edges in by ¼". Edgestitch the top folded edge of the pocket. (figure 8)

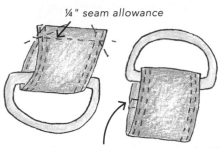

¼" seam allowance

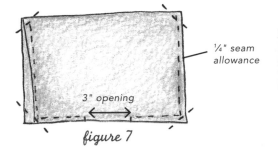

figure 5   Center seam along back side

Handle Tab with one D-ring   Handle Tab with two D-rings

1½"   1½"

1"   1"

¾"   ¾"

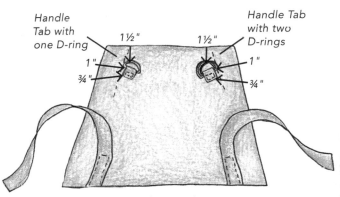

figure 6

¼" seam allowance

3" opening

figure 7

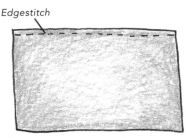

Edgestitch

figure 8

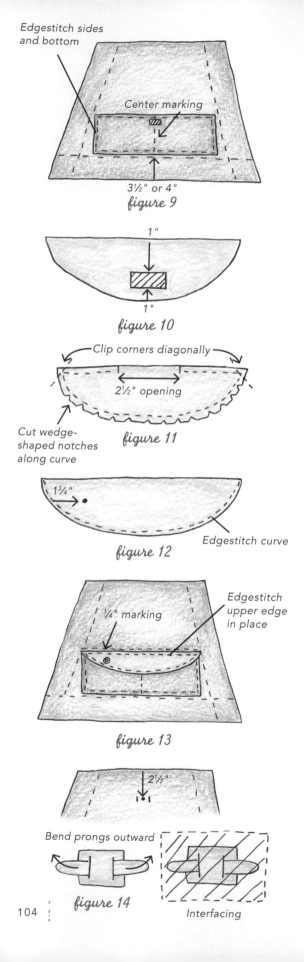

Edgestitch sides and bottom

Center marking

3½" or 4"

figure 9

1"

1"

figure 10

Clip corners diagonally

2½" opening

Cut wedge-shaped notches along curve

figure 11

1¾"

Edgestitch curve

figure 12

¼" marking

Edgestitch upper edge in place

figure 13

2½"

Bend prongs outward

figure 14

Interfacing

104

11 Cut a 1" piece of hook and loop tape. Apply the loop side to the center of the pocket, with the top edge of the tape ¼" down from the top edge of the pocket. Stitch around all sides of the tape to hold in place.

12 Mark down the center of the pocket. Place the pocket onto the front exterior bag piece without the handles, centered between the side markings and up from the bottom 3½" (for small) and 4" (for large). Pin in place and edgestitch the sides and bottom edges, then stitch down the center marking through the hook and loop tape to divide the pocket. (figure 9)

13 Cut two Media Pocket Flaps from Fabric C, as well as two from interfacing. Apply the interfacing to the wrong side of each flap. Apply the remaining half of the hook and loop tape to one of the flap pieces, centered and 1" from top and bottom edges of flap. (figure 10) Sew around edges of hook and loop tape.

14 Sew the flap right-sides together with a ¼" seam allowance, leaving a 2½" opening along the straight edge. Cut wedge-shaped notches from the curve to ease the seam in turning; clip corners diagonally. (figure 11) Turn the flap right-side out and press, fully turning out the corners and curve. Turn in ¼" along the opening.

15 Edgestitch the lower curved edge of the flap. Add the grommet for the earphone wire to the left side of the flap, centered up and down and 1¾" from the side edge. (figure 12) Then, apply the grommet. Refer to Essential Techniques for instructions (page 20).

16 Mark ¼" above the finished edge of the pocket. Align the straight-edge of the flap with this marking, centered above the pocket. Use the hook and loop tape to help center the flap. Edgestitch the upper edge of the flap in place. (figure 13)

17 Mark the center of the bag front 2½" down from the top edge. Center the twist portion of the closure horizontally over this center mark and mark prong placement. Use an awl to pierce the prong marks and enlarge those holes slightly with sharp, pointed scissors. Install the twist portion of the clasp on the right side of the bag front, following instructions in Step 11 on page 131. Prongs will be folded to the wrong side. (figure 14)

SEWING THE EXTERIOR BAG TOGETHER

1 To sew the exterior bag together, place the exterior front and back right-sides together with all edges even. Take care that the handles are tucked safely inside the layers. Pin the pieces together and sew along the side and bottom with a ½" seam allowance. (figure 15)

2 Lay the bag still wrong-side out on a flat surface and mark up from the bottom, 2" for *small* and 2½" for *large*, then again with the same measurement from the side at each bottom corner. Include the seam allowance in the measurement. Cut away on these markings to remove the bottom corners. Trim down the seam allowances to ¼". (figure 16)

3 Open out the bag at the cut areas and bring the bottom seam up to the side seam. Align them and pin the opening together at each corner. Sew across the corners with a ½" seam allowance. (figure 17) Trim the seam to ¼".

4 Briefly iron the bag to soften the Peltex, then turn right-side out. Press the seams, then fold the bag along the 2½" or 3" markings on the sides and crease it. Also fold along the bottom on the previous markings and press to crease. Bring the creased sides together on each side so that the side seams pleat inward. (figure 18) Clip the top of the bag layers together temporarily with clothespins or binder clips to hold the shape while working on other parts of the bag.

LINING & INTERIOR POCKET

1 For the lining, cut two rectangles from Fabric A and two from interfacing: *small*—14"×15"; *large*—17"×18". Fuse interfacing to wrong side of fabric. Trim rectangles into trapezoid shapes following the instructions in Step 3 on page 102.

2 For the zippered interior pocket, cut two squares and two strips from Fabric C:
Small: 8" squares and 8"×2" strips.
Large: 10" squares and 10"×2" strips.
Cut the same pieces from interfacing and apply to the wrong side of each fabric piece.

3 Center a 7" or 9" zipper on one of the 2" strips, with the right side of the zipper facing the right side of the strip. Align along one long side; use a zipper foot to stitch down that side. (figure 19)

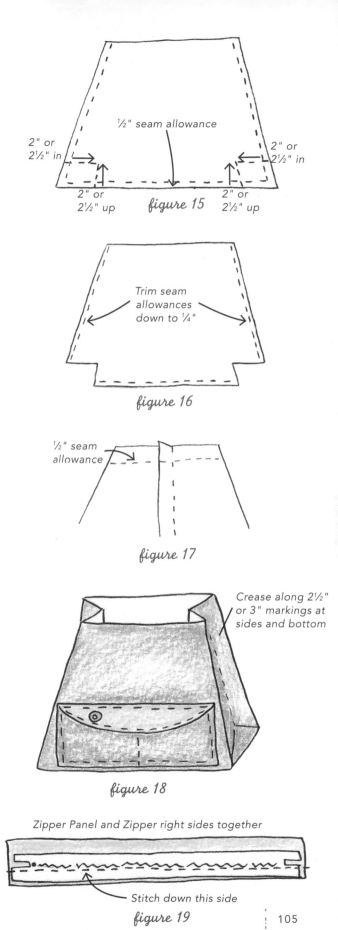

½" seam allowance

2" or 2½" in

2" or 2½" in

2" or 2½" up

2" or 2½" up

figure 15

Trim seam allowances down to ¼"

figure 16

½" seam allowance

figure 17

Crease along 2½" or 3" markings at sides and bottom

figure 18

Zipper Panel and Zipper right sides together

Stitch down this side

figure 19

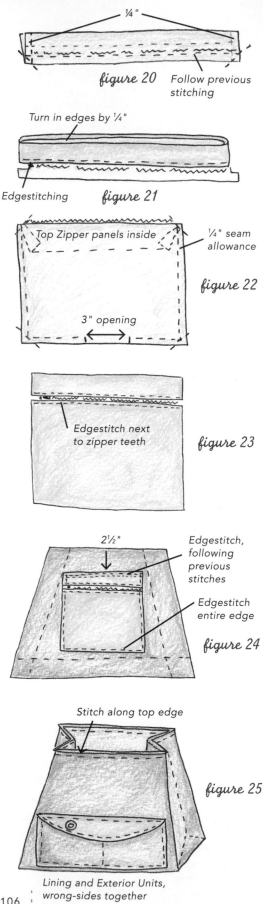

¼"

figure 20   Follow previous
stitching

Turn in edges by ¼"

Edgestitching   *figure 21*

Top Zipper panels inside   ¼" seam
allowance

figure 22

3" opening

Edgestitch next
to zipper teeth   *figure 23*

2½"   Edgestitch,
following
previous
stitches

Edgestitch
entire edge

figure 24

Stitch along top edge

figure 25

Lining and Exterior Units,
wrong-sides together

4 Lay the other 2" strip on top of the zipper unit along the sewn edge, right-sides together and edges even. Fold in the zipper tape on the unsewn side so it is not caught in the seam allowance. Follow the previous stitching to add this strip. While the strips are right-sides together with edges even, stitch across at each end, ¼" from the edges, leaving the long top edge unstitched. Trim the corners diagonally. (figure 20)

5 Turn zipper unit right side out and press flat, turning in the edges of the opening by ¼" and pressing to the inside. Edgestitch next to the zipper teeth. (figure 21)

6 Now apply the squares (8" or 10") to the opposite side of the zipper in the same manner as the strips were added. When stitching the squares together, be sure that the upper completed section does not get caught in the side seams, and leave a 3" opening for turning right-side out along the bottom edge. Trim the corners diagonally before turning. (figure 22)

7 Press the entire unit once the bottom section has been turned right-side out. Turn in the opening edges by ¼" and press in place. Edgestitch along the zipper teeth on the lower section. (figure 23)

8 Add the pocket to one of the lining pieces, 2½" down from the upper edge and centered from side to side. Pin in place and edgestitch all pocket edges. Edgestitch again along the upper zipper teeth, following previous stitching and topstitch on the upper section, ¼" below the upper edgestitching. (figure 24)

9 Sew the lining together just like you did for the exterior of the bag in Steps 1-3 of Sewing the Exterior Bag Together section, except use a ⅝" seam allowance. This will account for the bulk of the Peltex and the two united will fit together nicely. Don't forget to trim the seams once the corners have been cut away.

10 Press the lining, leaving it wrong-side out. Remove the clothespins from the main exterior bag and place the lining inside, *wrong* sides together with the zippered pocket against the handle side of the bag. Align the side seams and ease the lining into place so that the top edges are even with the exterior bag. If the lining extends ⅛" to ¼" beyond the top exterior bag edges, simply trim away the extra before sewing the layers together. Sew along the top edge of the bag to hold all of the layers together, ⅜" in from the raw edges. (figure 25)

BAG BINDING & GROMMETS

1 To bind the top edge of the bag, cut a strip 2¼" × the width of the fabric from Fabric B. Trim off the selvedges from each end, then press ½" to the wrong side along one of the narrow ends. Place the binding strip's right side against the inside top edge of the bag, and pin all the way around until reaching the starting point. Overlap by 1" and cut away any excess binding. Stitch the binding strip in place with a ½" seam allowance. (figure 26)

2 Open out the strip away from the bag and press. Fold the strip over the seam, turn the edge under by ¼" and press. Pin in place and edgestitch both the lower and upper edges. (figure 27)

3 For the grommet placement at the bag top for the drawstring, measure across the top edge of the bag between the side creases. (*Small* size should be close to 7" and the *large*, 9".) Mark the center at 3½" (*small*) or 4½" (*large*) as well as 1¾" (*small*) or 2¼" (*large*) to either side to divide the front and back into fourths. The sides will be approximately 4" (*small*) or 5" (*large*). Mark the center at 2" (*small*) or 2½" (*large*) and 1" (*small*) or 1¼" (*large*) on each side of center, respectively. (figure 28)

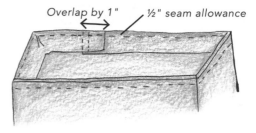

Overlap by 1"   ½" seam allowance

figure 26

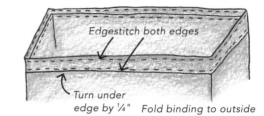

Edgestitch both edges

Turn under edge by ¼"   Fold binding to outside

figure 27

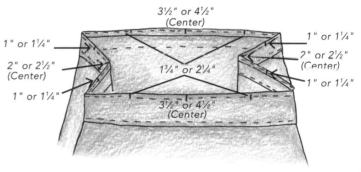

3½" or 4½" (Center)

1" or 1¼"   1" or 1¼"

2" or 2½" (Center)   2" or 2½" (Center)

1¾" or 2¼"   1" or 1¼"

1" or 1¼"

3½" or 4½" (Center)

figure 28

Zipper Charms

I love zipper charms! They're not always easy to find—I usually rely on the Internet to track them down—but they're worth it. Usually I like to show them off on the outside of a bag, but once in a while, that interior pocket can be surprisingly charming!

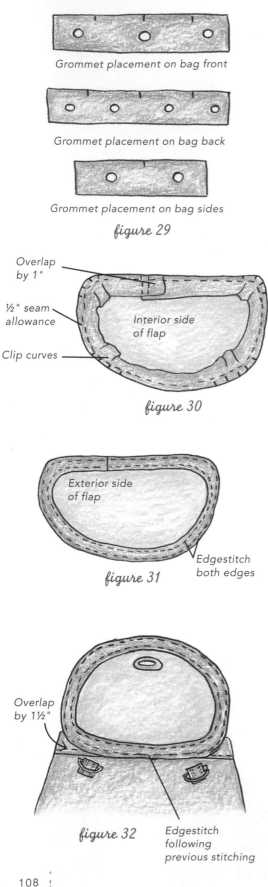

Grommet placement on bag front

Grommet placement on bag back

Grommet placement on bag sides

figure 29

Overlap
by 1"

½" seam
allowance

Interior side
of flap

Clip curves

figure 30

Exterior side
of flap

Edgestitch
both edges

figure 31

Overlap
by 1½"

Edgestitch
following
previous stitching

figure 32

4 The bag will use a total of 11 grommets. The bag back will need 4, the bag front will need 3, and the creased sides will need 2 each. On the front, mark the first grommet placement directly below the center marking. For all the others, center the grommets' placement between the markings. (figure 29) Once the grommet holes have been marked, follow the instructions in Essential Techniques (page 20) for adding grommets.

BAG FLAP & HANDLES

1 Cut two Bag Flaps from Fabric C and one from Peltex. Fuse one of the fabric pieces to the Peltex. Apply the remaining fabric piece (right-side facing up) to the other side of the Peltex using temporary spray adhesive. Stitch in ¼" from all edges.

2 Cut a 2½"-wide bias strip from Fabric B to bind the flap edge. Follow the instructions in Essential Techniques (pages 14-15) to create a strip that is approximately 24" (*small*) or 30" (*large*) long.

3 Starting with the pressed-under end, place the bias strip against the interior of the flap. Pin in place and overlap the ends by 1", cutting away any excess strip. Tuck the cut end into the pressed-under end. Stitch together with a ¼" seam allowance, clipping curves as necessary. (figure 30)

4 Open out the strip away from the flap and press. Fold the strip over the raw edges to the exterior side of the flap and press. Pin the lower folded edge in place and edgestitch, then edgestitch near the folded, finished edge. (figure 31)

5 To add the exterior portion of the twist latch to the flap, place the latch piece on the flap, centered horizontally and 1" up from the lower finished (curved) edge. Trace around the inside hole of the latch, and cut a hole. Carefully trim the hole until the latch fits nicely over the opening, then secure in place, following the instructions in Step 11 on page 131.

6 Place the straight bound edge of the bag flap over the binding on the back of the bag, with the inside of the flap facing the exterior of the bag back. Center the flap from side to side. The pieces should overlap by about 1½". Pin in place, then edgestitch the lower outside edge of flap (only), over previous stitching. Backstitch at the beginning and end of stitching. Be careful not to stitch so far up bag binding that the drawstring is compromised. (figure 32)

7 Once the flap is in place, fold the bag inward along the side creases and latch shut just to get an idea of how it will look.

8 For the next four steps, you'll need to refer to instructions for Installing a Double Loop Slider in Essential Techniques (pages 18-19). Start with the left handle. Feed the left handle through the D-ring above it. Slip the two-ring slider onto the handle, and then feed the handle-end through the *back* D-ring on the right side of the bag. (figure 33).

9 Pull up some slack on the slider so that the end of the left handle can be inserted around the center post of the slider. Fold the end of the handle under by ¼", then again by ¾" and pin the end in place. (figure 34) The handle should move freely to lengthen or shorten as desired.

10 Insert the right handle through the *front* D-ring, then slide on the double-loop slider. Insert the handle end through the D-ring on the left that already has the left handle through it. (figure 35) Pin this end of the handle in place like you did in Step 9.

11 Try the backpack on and work with the handles in the shortest position. If they seem too long to be comfortable on your shoulders, trim an equal amount from each handle to create to the appropriate length. Once you've determined a comfortable length, stitch the handle ends in place.

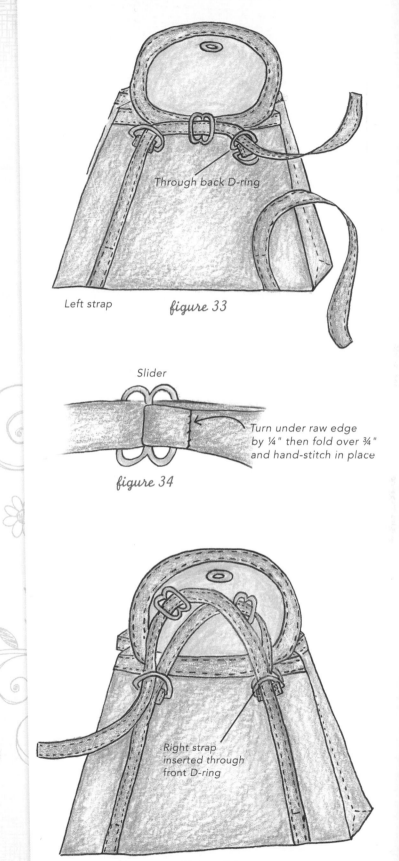

Through back D-ring

Left strap   *figure 33*

Slider

Turn under raw edge by ¼" then fold over ¾" and hand-stitch in place

figure 34

Right strap inserted through front D-ring

figure 35

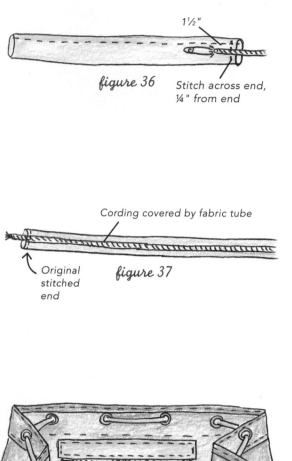

1½"

figure 36

Stitch across end,
¼" from end

Cording covered by fabric tube

figure 37

Original
stitched
end

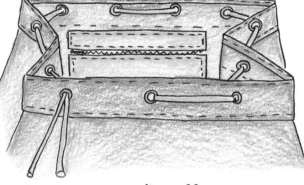

figure 38

12 The next step is to create the drawstring. Start by stitching across the cotton cording using a small tight zigzag stitch, about ½" in from the cut end. Place a medium-size safety pin through this stitching in the cording.

13 Cut a strip 1½" × the width of fabric from Fabric A. Fold the strip right-sides together, and stitch a ¼" seam along the long edge starting at one end and stopping 1½" before the other end. Place the safety-pin end of the cording inside the strip, about 1½" in from the end, as shown. Finish stitching the seam, then pivot and stitch across one end of the strip of the strip through the cording, enclosing the safety pin inside, about ¼" in from the end of the fabric. (figure 36)

14 Find the safety pin inside the tube and begin pushing it toward the open end, sliding the fabric along the cording. Smooth out the fabric as it covers the cording. When you've pulled the full length of the cording through, remove the safety pin. Trim the ends as desired. (figure 37)

15 Feed the cord through the grommets. (figure 38) (In the illustration, I've indicated feeding the drawstring through the grommets so that the ends are off-center, but you can refer to the photo on page 107 for another method.) Open out the bag and leave about 3" extra cording at each end. Tie an overhand knot at this point and trim away the rest of the cording. Tighten down the knots by pulling on them.

16 To close the bag, pull the drawstring. Fold over the flap and turn the latch to close.

Convertible Straps

When the straps are completed, the rings should allow you adjust to the straps as you please. You can carry your creation as a handbag (far left, and below) or wear it as a backpack (left).

MULTI-TASKER BAG

The Multi-Tasker bag is just that—a bag for toting around miscellaneous stuff for travel, crafts or everyday use. The size and structure of this bag make it easy to keep everything organized and the zippered top ensures that nothing will fall out. The exterior media pocket is perfect for your iPod or other mp3 player as well as additional pockets for stashing a cell phone and other items. I even added a loop to the exterior along the top edge for attaching your keys if you like! This bag lends itself well to choosing bold fabrics with prominent motifs along with several coordinates.

my initial sketch

By customizing the pockets, you could easily have the zippered exterior pocket featured in the diaper bag version as part of a bag for scrapbooking or sewing to hold notions and other tools. Feel free to customize the interior pockets, dividing them in any way that would be of the greatest use to you. *The sweet flowers featured with these bags are a free tutorial on my blog at blog.SewSerendipity.com.*

materials list

Fabric

Fabric A—Bag Exterior and Large Exterior Pocket: 1⅛ yard

Fabric B—Exterior Side Pockets, Media Pocket and Exterior Zipper Panel: ½ yard

Fabric C—Media Pocket flap, binding for all exterior pockets and Interior pockets: ½ yard

Fabric D—Binding at top edge, Handle Tabs, Handle and key ring loop: ⅓ yard

Fabric E—Lining and Interior Zipper Panel: ⅞ yard

All yardage based on 45"- wide cotton fabrics.

Other Materials

1⅝ yards Peltex one-sided fusible interfacing

3 yards fusible interfacing for light- to medium-weight fabrics

One 14" separating sport zipper

Two 2" wide square rings (handle)

One 1" swivel clasp (key ring loop)

One ⅜" metal grommet (media pocket)

1" piece of ¾"-wide hook and loop tape (media pocket closure)

Matching polyester thread

Heavy-duty machine needle (such as for denim)

Zipper foot

Rotary cutter, ruler and mat

Sharp, pointed scissors

Removable marking pencil

Super glue

Needle-nose pliers

Finished Dimensions

12" × 14" wide × 5" deep, with a handle up to 40" in length

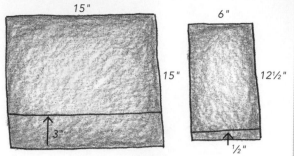

15"

6"

15"

12½"

3"

½"

figure 1

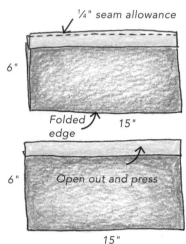

¼" seam allowance

6"

Folded edge

15"

6"

Open out and press

15"

figure 2

Edgestitching

6"

15"

figure 3

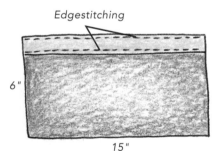

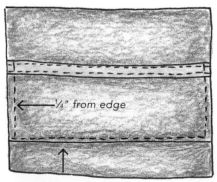

¼" from edge

3" marking   figure 4

LAYOUT & CUTTING

The pattern piece for the Media Pocket Flap is provided (sheet 5). All other pieces are cut according to measurements given in the instructions using a rotary cutter, ruler and mat. All seam allowances are ½", unless otherwise stated.

PREPARE THE EXTERIOR BAG PIECES

1 From Fabric A and Peltex, cut two 15" squares and two rectangles, 6" wide × 12½" tall. Fussy cut as desired. Keep in mind that you'll be adding pockets to both sides.

2 Apply the Peltex to the wrong side of each fabric piece.

3 On the 15" squares, measure 3" up from the lower edge and mark a line across the piece. On the 6"×12½" rectangles, measure ½" up from the lower edge and mark a line. (figure 1)

LARGE EXTERIOR POCKET

If you are making the Diaper Bag variation, replace this section with Exterior Pockets–Elastic and Zippered from pages 124-126.

1 For the large exterior pocket, cut one 12" tall × 15" wide rectangle from Fabric A and one from fusible interfacing. Fussy cut as needed. Fuse the interfacing to the wrong side of the fabric.

2 Fold the pocket in half and press wrong-sides together, so that it measures 6"×15." Press.

3 For pocket binding, cut a strip 3" × the width of fabric from Fabric C. Trim off the selvedges, then fold the strip in half lengthwise with wrong-sides together and press.

4 Pin the raw edges of the strip along the top 15"-wide raw edge of the pocket with right sides together and raw edges aligned. (This will be the inside of the pocket so keep the fabric's design motif in mind.) Stitch with a ¼" seam allowance. Trim off excess, open out and press. Open out the strip away from the pocket and press. (figure 2)

5 Fold the strip over the seam to the other side of the pocket and press. Edgestitch both edges of the strip to hold it in place. (figure 3)

6 Add the pocket to one of the 15" squares, with the folded edge of the pocket along the 3" marked line and side edges even. Pin in place and edgestitch the lower edge, then stitch ¼" in from the sides. (figure 4)

EXTERIOR SIDE POCKETS & HANDLE TABS

1   For the exterior side pockets, cut two rectangles each measuring 7" wide × 12½" tall from Fabric B and two from fusible interfacing. Fuse the interfacing to the wrong side of each pocket piece.

2   Fold the pocket pieces in half with wrong sides together and press, so that they measure 7" × 6¼".

3   Cut a strip 2¼" × the width of fabric from Fabric C for binding.

4   Pin the raw edges of the strip along the raw edge of the 6¼" side of the pocket. (This side will be the inside of the pocket.) Trim off excess. Stitch with a ¼" seam allowance. Open out the strip away from the pocket and press. (figure 5)

5   Fold the strip over the seam to the other side of the pocket and press. Edgestitch both edges of the strip to hold it in place. (figure 6)

6   Fold the pocket in half lengthwise with the exterior side facing out. At the lower edge, measure in ½" from the fold, and stitch vertically from that point, about ¾" up. This will form a pleat so that the pocket has depth. (figure 7)

7   Unfold the pocket and open up the pleat so that its fold is centered on the stitching. Press, then edgestitch the exterior pressed area of the pleat in place. (figure 8)

8   Repeat steps 4 through 7 for the remaining pocket.

9   Add the pockets to the bag end pieces, along the ½" marking on the lower edge. Align the side edges and pin in place. Edgestitch the sides and lower edge of the pockets. (figure 9) There will be slack in the upper finished edge; this allows you enough room to carry bulkier items.

10   For the handle tabs, cut two 3" × 16" strips from Fabric D and two from fusible interfacing. Fuse the interfacing to the wrong side of the fabric strips, then follow the instructions for making handles in Essential Techniques (pages 16-17).

11   Add some additional lines of stitching to the tabs, about ¼" apart until there are six lines of stitching across the width of the piece. (figure 10) Cut the tab unit into two 8" lengths.

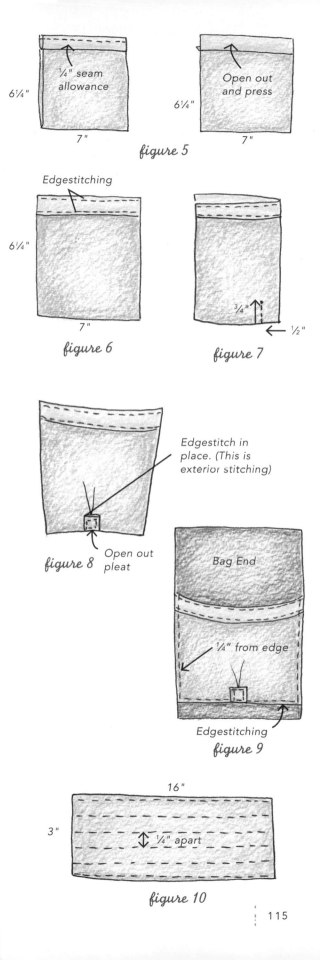

6¼"   ¼" seam allowance   7"

6¼"   Open out and press   7"

figure 5

Edgestitching

6¼"   7"

figure 6

¾"   ½"

figure 7

Edgestitch in place. (This is exterior stitching)

figure 8   Open out pleat

Bag End

¼" from edge

Edgestitching

figure 9

16"

3"   ¼" apart

figure 10

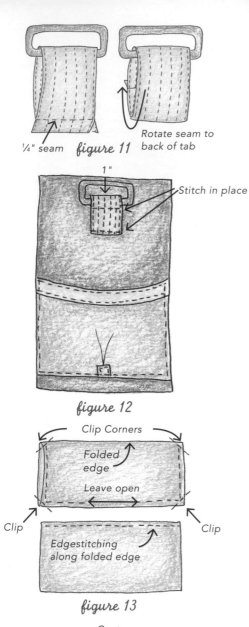

¼" seam   *figure 11*   Rotate seam to back of tab

1"

Stitch in place

figure 12

Clip Corners

Folded edge

Leave open

Clip   Clip

Edgestitching along folded edge

figure 13

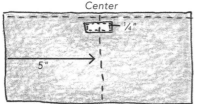

Center

¼"

5"

figure 14

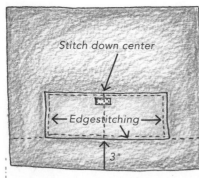

Stitch down center

Edgestitching

3"

116

figure 15

12 Place one of the tabs through one of the square rings and fold in half. Stitch together with a ¼" seam allowance. Rotate the seam so that it is centered along the back of the tab loop. (figure 11)

13 Place the tab onto the bag side piece, 1" down from the top edge and centered side to side. Edgestitch along the bottom edge of the tab, then stitch along the side of the tab up close to the hardware. Pivot and stitch across the tab below the hardware, backstitching to reinforce. Pivot and stitch down the remaining side. (figure 12)

14 Repeat for the remaining tab piece.

MEDIA POCKET

1 For the media pocket, cut one 10½" square from Fabric B and one from interfacing. Apply the interfacing to the wrong side of the square.

2 Fold the square in half with right sides together. Stitch along the sides and bottom with a ¼" seam allowance, leaving a 3" opening along the bottom edge. Clip the corners diagonally and turn the pocket right-side out. Press, turning in opening edges by ¼". Edgestitch the top folded edge of the pocket. (figure 13)

3 Cut one 1" square of hook and loop tape. Apply the loop side to the center of the pocket, with the top edge of the tape ¼" down from the top edge of the pocket. Stitch around all sides to hold in place. Mark a line down the center of the pocket at 5". (figure 14)

4 Place the pocket onto the remaining exterior bag piece, centered from side to side along the 3" marked line at the bottom. Pin in place and edgestitch the sides and bottom edge of the pocket, then stitch down the center line over the hook and loop tape to divide the pocket. (figure 15)

5 Cut two exterior Media Pocket flaps from Fabric C as well as two from interfacing. Apply the interfacing to the wrong side of each flap. Apply the remaining half of the hook and loop tape to one of the flap pieces, centered and 1" from top and bottom edges of flap. Sew around edges of tape.

6 Sew the flap right-sides together with a ¼" seam allowance, leaving a 2½" opening along the straight edge of the flap. Wedge-cut notches into the curve to ease the seam in turning, and clip corners diagonally. Turn the flap right-side out (fully turning out the corners and curve), then turn in ¼" along the opening and press. (figure 16)

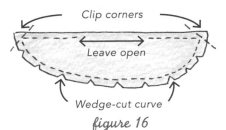

figure 16

7 Edgestitch the lower, curved edge of the flap. Place the grommet (for the earphone wire) on the left side of the flap, centered and 1¾" from the side edge of the flap to the center of the grommet. Trace around the inside of the grommet. (figure 17) Apply the grommet following the instructions in Essential Techniques (page 20).

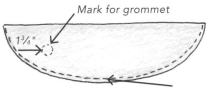

figure 17 Edgestitching

8 Use a ruler to place a mark ¼" above the finished edge of the pocket. Align the top of the flap with this marking, centered above the pocket. Use the hook and loop tape to help center the pocket flap. Edgestitch the upper edge of the flap in place. (figure 18)

SEWING THE BAG TOGETHER

1 Sew the exterior of the bag together alternating the large exterior bag pieces with the narrower bag end pieces. Align the *top* edges of the bag pieces, as the end pieces are shorter. Place pieces right-sides together and sew, starting at the top edge and *stopping ½" before the lower edge of the shorter end pieces.* (figure 19)

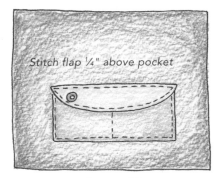

figure 18

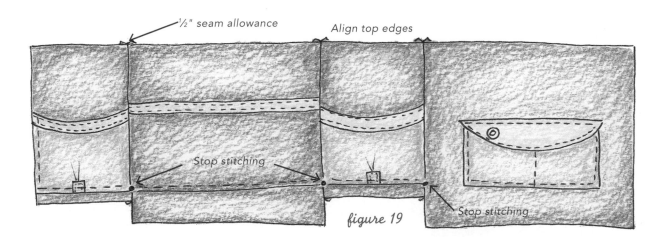

figure 19

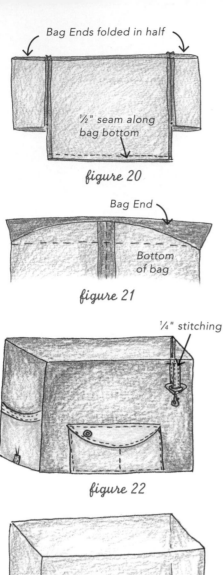

Bag Ends folded in half

½" seam along
bag bottom

figure 20

Bag End

Bottom
of bag

figure 21

¼" stitching

figure 22

Details of exterior
omitted to illustrate
Peltex placement

Peltex (inside bag)

figure 23

2 Stitch each seam twice to reinforce the stitching. *For the diaper bag version, take care to follow the previous stitching where the zippers are attached.* Trim down the seams above the ½" marking to ¼" at the lower edge and press the seams open.

3 Once all four seams have been stitched twice, fold the end pieces in half so that the two larger bag exterior pieces are aligned along the lower edge of the bag exterior (but not bag ends). Stitch this lower edge together with a ½" seam allowance. (figure 20) Stitch again to reinforce. Trim the seam allowance down to ¼", then press the seam open.

4 To make the bottom corners that form the shape of the bag, bring the bag exterior bottom and bag end pieces together, centering the bottom seam of the exterior on the narrow bag end pieces. Pin in place. This will seem awkward, but *resist* the urge to do any clipping—you'll just end up creating a hole. These two pieces *won't* lie flush against one another, but will sew together with a good result. Before stitching, refer to the illustration to make sure everything looks right. (figure 21)

5 Stitch across the end twice and double-check the seam by peeking inside the bag. When you're certain that it is sewn together securely, trim the seam. Briefly steam the bag to soften the Peltex, then turn it right-side out and press following the instructions in the Essential Techniques (page 22). Be sure to crease all seams at the corners as well as the lower edges where the pockets meet the bottom of the bag. *Test the zippers on the diaper bag variation to be sure that they zip and unzip nicely.*

6 To add the key loop to the bag, cut one 2½"×6" strip from Fabric D and one from fusible interfacing. Fuse the interfacing to the wrong side of the fabric. Fold the strip in half lengthwise wrong sides together and press. Open out the strip and fold the long edges toward the center by ¼" and press, then fold in half once more and press. Edgestitch both long edges.

7 Place the strip through the loop end of the swivel clasp and fold the strip in half. Add the loop to the exterior of the bag on the media pocket side toward the right with the loop raw edges aligned with bag raw edges. Stitch through all layers ¼" from the raw edge. (figure 22)

8 For added reinforcement, an additional piece of Peltex can be added to the interior of the bag. Cut a rectangle 5"×14" and place inside the bag with the fusible side facing the bag interior. You may need to trim off the corners to make it fit nicely. Place your iron inside the bag and press to activate the adhesive of the Peltex to secure it in place. (figure 23)

BAG LINING & INTERIOR POCKETS

1 For the bag lining, cut two 15" tall × 20" wide rectangles each from Fabric E and fusible interfacing. Fuse the interfacing to the wrong side of the fabric. You can make the interior pockets two ways: flat (steps 2-5) or with an elasticized top (steps 6-10).

2 For the flat interior pocket, cut one rectangle measuring 12½" tall × 14½" wide from Fabric C and one from fusible interfacing. Fuse the interfacing to the wrong side of fabric.

3 Fold the pocket in half with right sides together so that it measures 6¼" × 14½". Stitch with a ¼" seam allowance around the three sides, leaving an opening for turning along the lower edge. Clip the corners. (figure 24)

4 Turn right-side out and press. Edgestitch along the upper folded edge. (figure 25)

5 Place the pocket on one of the lining pieces, 3¼" above the lower edge and centered from side to side. Edgestitch the side and lower edges of the pocket in place. Mark a line down the center of the pocket at 7", then 3½" to one side of that to divide the pocket into three parts. Stitch down the marked lines. (figure 26) For another flat pocket on the remaining lining piece, repeat steps 2 through 5.

6 For the elasticized interior pocket, cut one rectangle measuring 12½" tall ×18" wide from Fabric C and from fusible interfacing. Fuse the interfacing to the wrong side of the fabric.

7 Fold the pocket in half right-sides together so that it measures 6¼" ×18". Mark ½" down from the top folded edge on both narrow sides (for the elastic casing). Beginning at the marking, stitch around the pocket edges with a ¼" seam allowance. Leave a 3" opening along the bottom edge for turning right-side out. (figure 27)

8 Clip the corners and turn right-side out. Press. Stitch across the top ½" down from and parallel to the folded edge to create the elastic casing. Mark a line down the center of the pocket at 9", then again at 4½" from each end to divide into four equal parts. (figure 28)

9 Cut a piece of elastic 11" long and insert into casing just until the end of the elastic is barely inside the casing. Stitch at one end across the casing and over the elastic, ¼" in from the side. Continue pulling the elastic through casing until the remaining end is even with the other end of the casing, then stitch in place. (figure 29)

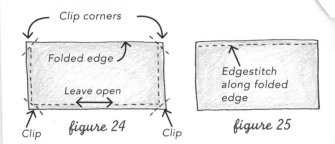

figure 24

figure 25

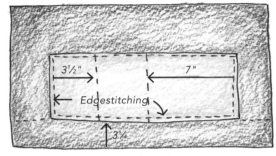

figure 26

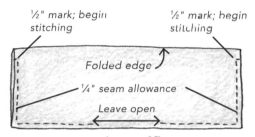

figure 27

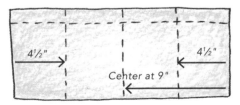

figure 28

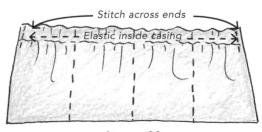

figure 29

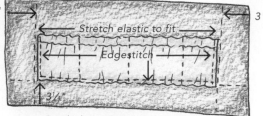

Stitch down divisions in pocket

figure 30

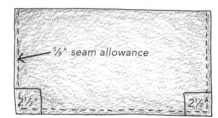

⅝" seam allowance

figure 31

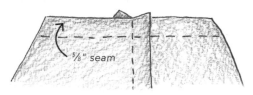

⅝" seam

figure 32

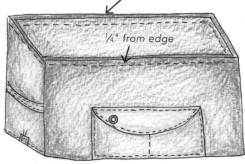

Trim away an excess liner as necessary

¼" from edge

Key loop omitted for illustrative purposes

figure 33

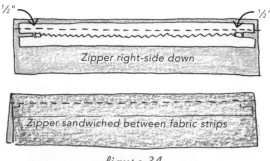

½" ½"

Zipper right-side down

Zipper sandwiched between fabric strips

figure 34

10 Make gathers (page 13) along the bottom of the pocket. Distribute the gathers evenly until the bottom of the pocket measures 14". Press lightly. Mark in 3" on each side of the lining piece and make a vertical line. Mark a horizontal line 3¼" up from the lower edge. Place the pocket along the line that's 3¼" from the bottom edge, with the side edges of the pockets lined up on the 3" marked lines. Stretch the elastic to accommodate, pin and edgestitch sides and lower edge of the pocket in place. (figure 30)

11 Sew the lining pieces right-sides together along the side and bottom edges with a ⅝" seam allowance. Leave the seam allowance intact and mark a 2½" square at both bottom corners. Include the seam allowance in the measurement. (figure 31)

12 Cut away the corners on the markings, then trim the seam allowance to ¼". Bring the side seam to the bottom seam, aligning the raw edges at each corner and matching seam lines. Sew across with a ⅝" seam allowance (figure 32) then trim down to ¼". Repeat on other corner.

13 Place the lining inside the exterior of the bag with wrong sides together. Ease the lining into the corners and really work with your hands to smooth the layers together. If the lining extends beyond the exterior by ¼" or so at the top, allow it. It's more important that the two layers fit together nicely. If the lining needs to be trimmed, do that now. Pin along the top edge, then stitch ¼" away from raw edges to secure all layers together. (figure 33)

ZIPPER PANELS, BINDING & HANDLES

1 For the zipper panels, cut two strips 3" wide × 15" long from Fabric B (exterior zipper panel) and from Fabric E (interior zipper panel) and four from fusible interfacing. Fuse the interfacing to the wrong side of each strip.

2 Separate the zipper and work with one half at a time. Center the right side of the zipper against the right side of a Fabric B piece with the raw edge of the fabric against the edge of the zipper tape. Use a zipper foot to stitch the two together ½" from the edge. Place the Fabric E strip over zipper and Fabric B so that the fabrics are right-sides together with zipper sandwiched between. Follow the previous stitching to join all layers. (figure 34)

3 While the fabrics are still right sides together, stitch across the short ends, ½" in from raw edge. Trim the corners diagonally. (figure 35) Turn right-side out and press flat, then edgestitch and topstitch next to the zipper with the Fabric B side facing up. (figure 36)

4 Repeat Steps 2 and 3 for the remaining half of the zipper. Zip the zipper together again and check to be sure that the ends of fabric line up. If you have problems zipping (if you placed the teeth too close to the fabric, for instance), you may need to remove it and start over.

5 Unzip once more. Place one half of the zipper on one side of the bag with the lining side of the zipper panel against the lining side of the bag. Center the zipper panel on the bag exterior between the side seams with the raw edges together and pin. Stitch the zipper panel to the bag, ¼" in from the raw edges. (figure 37) Repeat for the other half of the zipper panel. Zip up the zipper to be sure that it works properly.

6 To bind the top of the bag, cut a strip 3" by the width of fabric from Fabric D. Trim off the selvedges, then fold the strip in half lengthwise wrong-sides together and press.

7 Open out the strip and fold ½" to the wrong side along one of the narrow ends and press. (figure 38) Fold the strip lengthwise again and press.

8 With the zipper unzipped, pin the raw edge of the binding to the top of the bag along the lining, starting with the pressed-under edge of binding. Pin all the way around until the beginning of the binding is reached. Allow an extra 1" for overlap and trim away the rest. (figure 39)

9 Open out the pressed-under end of binding and place the cut end inside to conceal it. (figure 40) Pin in place, then stitch around the top of the bag with a ⅜" seam allowance. (figure 41)

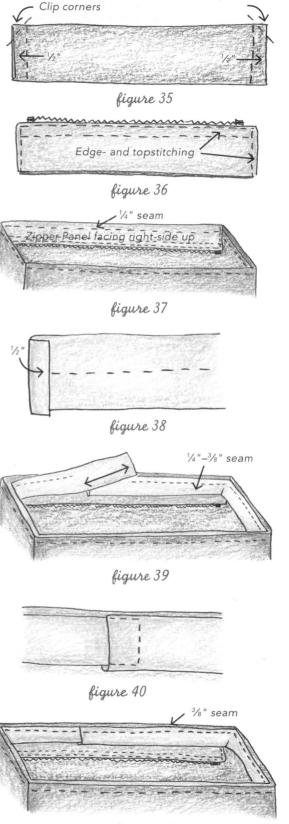

Clip corners

½"   ½"

figure 35

Edge- and topstitching

figure 36

¼" seam

Zipper Panel facing right-side up

figure 37

½"

figure 38

¼"–⅜" seam

figure 39

figure 40

⅜" seam

figure 41

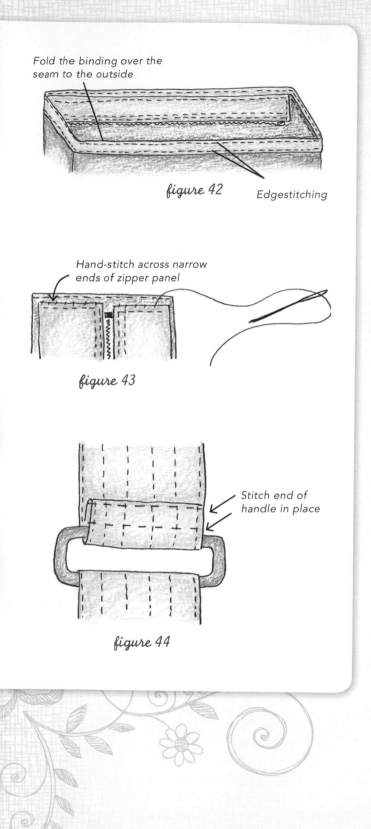

Fold the binding over the seam to the outside

figure 42

Edgestitching

Hand-stitch across narrow ends of zipper panel

figure 43

Stitch end of handle in place

figure 44

10 Fold the binding over the seam to the outside of the bag and press. The stitching along the top of the bag should be completely concealed. If not, trim the seam down slightly and try again. Pin the binding in place, then edgestitch both edges. (figure 42)

11 Check the zipper once more to be sure that it is fully operational. With needle and thread, hand-stitch the narrow ends of the zipper panel in place onto the narrow ends of the lining. This will keep the panel from dropping to the inside of the bag while unzipped. (figure 43)

12 Once the stitching is complete, use some super glue to secure the separating part of the zipper so that it does not come apart during use.

13 For the handles, cut two strips $3\frac{1}{2}$" × the width of fabric from Fabric D and five strips $3\frac{1}{2}$" × the width of interfacing from the fusible interfacing. Fuse the interfacing to the wrong side of the fabric, then follow the instructions for making the handles in Essential Techniques (pages 16-17).

14 Once the handles have been completed, add lines of topstitching, resulting in six rows of stitches. (See Step 11 from Exterior Side Pockets and Handle Tabs, page 115).

15 Place the ends of the handle through the square rings and pin in place. Slip the bag over your shoulder and adjust the length as you like, cutting away any excess handle as desired. Turn under the ends twice by $\frac{1}{2}$", then edge and topstitch them in place. (figure 44)

If you are creating the Diaper Bag Variation, move on to the Removable Changing Pad Instructions on page 126 to complete the bag.

DIAPER BAG VARIATION

I have also included a variation for this bag that makes it into a very clever diaper bag for the stylish mom on the go with a removable changing pad built right into the bag's exterior.

materials list

Fabric

Fabric B— Additional yardage for changing pad exterior: ⅝ yard

Fabric D—Additional yardage for bias trim on changing pad: ¼ yard

Fusible fleece—changing pad and exterior zippered pocket: ⅓ yard

Polyurethane laminate (PUL)—for changing pad: ⅝ yard

Additional Tools

Two 12" standard zippers

⅜" wide elastic—diaper and interior pockets: 1 yard

1½" wide hook and loop tape—changing pad: 9"

Teflon-coated foot—*may be necessary if working with PUL fabric*

Walking foot—*an alternative option for working with PUL fabric*

PUL

Polyurethane laminate (PUL) is a 56"-wide laminated knit fabric that is wipeable and soft. It's perfect for the gathered pockets inside the exterior pocket as well as for the changing pad. It might not be readily available, but it's worth searching out, especially for a diaper bag. Take care when ironing; it can melt if you don't use a pressing cloth.

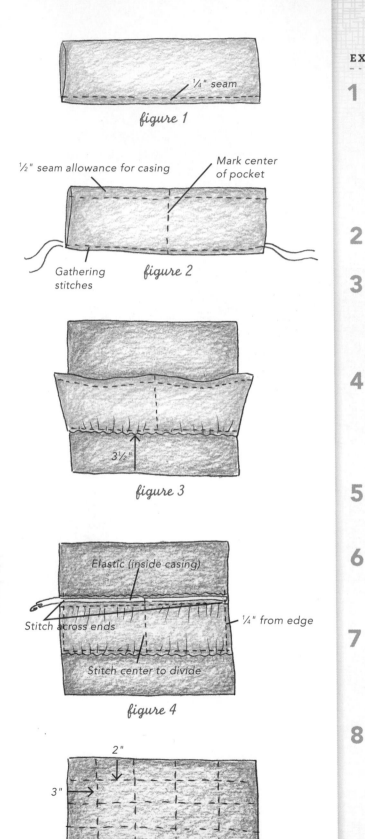

figure 1

¼" seam

½" seam allowance for casing

Mark center of pocket

Gathering stitches

figure 2

3½"

figure 3

Elastic (inside casing)

Stitch across ends

¼" from edge

Stitch center to divide

figure 4

2"

3"

figure 5

EXTERIOR POCKETS—ELASTIC AND ZIPPERED

1 The elasticized pocket is concealed inside the zippered exterior pocket on the outside of the bag. To make this pocket, cut a 12½"×20" rectangle from the PUL fabric. Fold the fabric in half with the laminated sides together to measure 6¼"×20". Stitch the long edges together with a ¼" seam allowance, then turn right-side out. Place the seam along one side. Using a pressing cloth on top of the fabric, gently press the piece flat. (figure 1)

2 Complete a line of stitching ½" from the folded edge to form the casing for the elastic.

3 Mark down the center of the pocket unit at 10". Using a long straight machine stitch, complete a line of stitching along the seam line of the pocket unit. Leave long tails of thread at each end so that the pocket can be gathered. (figure 2)

4 Add the pocket unit onto one of the 15" exterior squares on the fabric side. Place the bottom edge of the pocket 3½" up from the lower edge with the sides even. Pull the gathering threads carefully until the pocket unit matches in size with the side of the bag. Pin in place and edgestitch the lower edge of the pocket. (figure 3)

5 Cut a piece of elastic 12" long and insert into casing along the top of the pocket. Stitch at both ends, ¼" in from the side.

6 Slightly pull the pocket until the sides line up with the bag side and pin together. Stitch the sides of the pocket in place, ¼" in from the side edges. Also stitch down the center of the pocket to divide it. (figure 4)

7 Cut a 10"×15" rectangle each from Fabric A, PUL and fusible fleece. Apply the fleece to the wrong side of Fabric A. Layer the PUL on the other side of the fleece with the laminated side facing up. Pin together in a few places.

8 On the Fabric A side, mark quilting lines at every 3" along the 15" side and at every 2" along the 10" side. Use a walking foot with the PUL fabric against the feed dogs to quilt. (figure 5)

9 Trim the rectangle to 9" × 14", trimming down ½" along each side to keep the quilting lines centered.

10 Use an overlock stitch or serge the 9" edges. Mark ½" in along these edges; you'll use this as a fold line to fold back when adding the zippers to each side. (figure 6)

11 To add the zippers, position the top stop of the zipper ½" down from the top edge of the zippered pocket unit along one of the 9" ends. Use a zipper foot to sew in place. Repeat for the remaining zipper on the other side. The zipper will extend beyond the edge and will be trimmed away in the next step. (figure 7)

12 Once the zippers have been added, stitch back and forth several times over each zipper even with the raw edge of the diaper pad unit. Test the zipper to be sure it stops at the stitching, then cut away the excess amount of zipper.

13 Bind the lower edge of the zippered pocket unit by cutting a strip 2¼" by the width of fabric from Fabric C. Trim off the selvedges, then fold the strip in half lengthwise wrong-sides together and press.

14 Pin the binding to the PUL side of the zippered pocket unit along the lower edge, starting at the outer edge of the zipper tape. Stitch together with a ¼" seam allowance. (figure 8)

15 Open out the strip and fold over the seam to the fabric side of the pocket unit. Pin in place after pressing. Edgestitch both edges of the binding in place. (figure 9)

16 Use the same method to bind the upper edge of the zippered pocket unit, *except* open out the strip and fold ¼" to the wrong side at each end of the binding so that the ends are neatly finished. Start where the zipper is joined to the Pocket Unit and continue all the way across to the other zipper. (figure 10)

17 Fold the binding over the seam to the fabric side. Press and edgestitch in place. (figure 11)

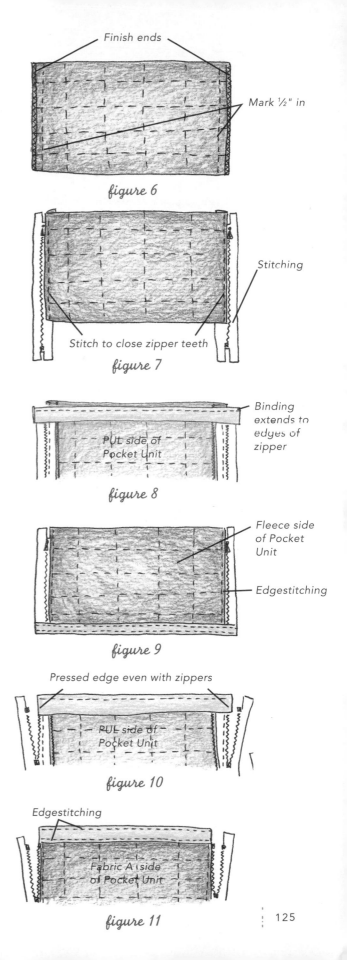

figure 6

Finish ends

Mark ½" in

figure 7

Stitching

Stitch to close zipper teeth

figure 8

PUL side of Pocket Unit

Binding extends to edges of zipper

figure 9

Fleece side of Pocket Unit

Edgestitching

figure 10

Pressed edge even with zippers

PUL side of Pocket Unit

figure 11

Edgestitching

Fabric A side of Pocket Unit

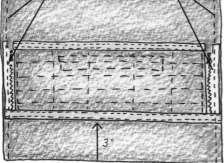

Hook and loop tape

PUL Side
(Quilting lines not shown)

figure 12

"Implied" stitching line of zipper tape lined up with ½" marking

3"

figure 13

Slightly round corners

figure 14

¼"

PUL Side of changing pad

figure 15

18 Add the soft loop of the hook and loop tape piece to the PUL side of the pocket unit along the upper edge, just below the binding. (figure 12)

19 On the exterior bag piece with the PUL pockets added, mark in ½" on each side. Pin the zippered pocket unit to the bag exterior *over* the PUL elasticized pocket with the lower bound edge of the zippered pocket along the 3" marking and the *implied* stitching lines for the remaining zipper tapes lined up with the ½" marking. This will be slightly inside the raw side edges. (figure 13)

20 Stitch zipper in place using a zipper foot. Use a regular foot to edgestitch the lower edge of the pocket in place, through the binding, along the 3" marking.

Return to the General Instructions starting at Sewing the Bag Together (page 117).

REMOVABLE CHANGING PAD

1 For the removable changing pad, cut one 14"×20" rectangle each from Fabric B, PUL and fusible fleece.

2 Add the fusible fleece to the wrong side of the fabric and fuse in place.

3 Place the PUL on the fleece side with the laminated side facing out. Pin the layers together in a few places. Mark diagonal quilting lines on the pad, 2¼" apart.

4 Using a walking foot with the PUL against the feed dogs of your machine; quilt the layers together over the marked lines.

5 Once the quilting is complete, trim down the piece to 12"×18" and slightly round the corners. (figure 14)

6 Create the binding from the additional ¼" yard of Fabric D. Cut a series of 2¼" wide bias strips and piece together according to the instructions in Essential Techniques for Bias Strips (pages 14-15).

7 Pin the bias strip to the PUL side of the changing pad along one of the narrow ends, beginning with the pressed-under edge of the strip. Leave the first couple of inches free and stitch around with a ¼" seam allowance. When you reach the starting point, trim the excess binding, leaving an extra 1" for tucking inside the folded edge of the binding. (figure 15)

8 Tuck the cut edge of the binding inside the pressed edge and finish stitching. (figure 16)

9 Fold the binding around to the fabric side of the pad, and press. Edgestitch the folded edge of the binding in place. (figure 17)

10 Add the remaining 9" piece of hook and loop tape to one of the narrow ends on the fabric side, just below the binding. Attach it to the hook and loop tape on the zippered pocket. (figure 18) Fold the pad into thirds so that it fits just inside the pocket, and zip up the pocket.

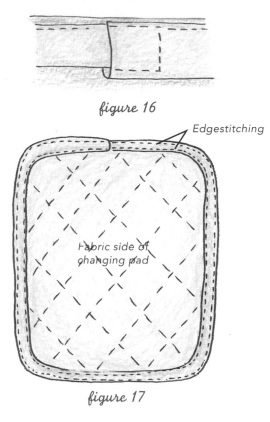

figure 16

Edgestitching

Fabric side of changing pad

figure 17

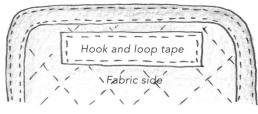

Hook and loop tape

Fabric side

figure 18

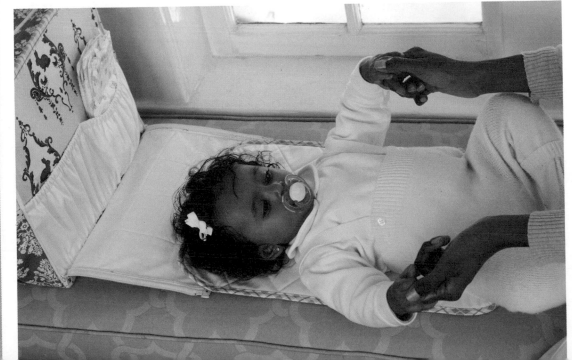

LAPTOP MESSENGER BAG

The Laptop Messenger Bag is the perfect way to express your personal style, yet stay organized while carrying your computer, business correspondence and all of your other electronic gadgets. There's even a pocket with a grommet—perfect for your media player and headphones. Everything is held in place with the large flap featuring a metal switch lock closure, plus the handles are long enough to accommodate carrying the bag comfortably on your shoulder. The interior features a quilted removable pouch with a zipper closure, suitable for computers with up to a 15" monitor. Because the pouch is centered in the bag, it stands without tipping once the computer is loaded. Other features of the interior include a front storage space for small items and a larger pocket in the back section to keep files organized. With a bag that does so much, you'll be an instant success!

my initial sketch

To make this bag uniquely your own, try mixing the fabrics around more or adding more interior pockets to fit your individual needs. You can also use a different type of latch on the flap for a different look. Use your imagination and think out of the box!

materials list

Fabric

Fabric A—bag exterior, lining, exterior media pocket and exterior of computer pouch: 1¾ yards

Fabric B—handles, flap binding, bag binding, interior pockets, lining for computer pouch and binding for computer pouch: 1¾ yards

Fabric C—media pocket flap, main bag flap, and zipper panel for computer pouch: 1 yard

All yardage based on 45"- wide cotton fabrics.

Other Materials

2⅛ yards one-sided fusible stabilizer (Peltex 71)

2⅜ yards fusible interfacing for light- to mid-weight fabrics

2½ yards ¾"-wide hook and loop tape

One 18"–20" zipper (not sport weight)

One 1"×⅜" metal twist latch

Two 12"×18" pieces high loft polyester batting (¾" thickness)

Rotary cutter, ruler and mat

Sharp, pointed scissors

Removable marking pencil

Thread to match fabrics

Monofilament or clear thread

One decorative zipper charm

One ⅜" metal grommet

Temporary adhesive spray

Heavy-duty machine needle (such as for denim)

Finished Dimensions

12½"×15"×5" deep at the base, 3" deep at the opening
The handles have a 9" or 12" drop.

The interior computer pouch measures 11"×15"×1¼" deep.

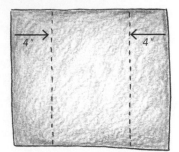

figure 1

Handles centered on 4" marking

figure 2

Making Handles for a 12" Drop

To make the handles with a 12" drop, the construction is the same, but the number of strips changes. Cut an extra strip by the width of fabric and trim off the selvedge edges. Cut two of the strips in half, rather than quartering them. Add the half strips to each of the four remaining full-length strips. Cut two additional strips of interfacing to accommodate the length, overlapping as needed. Trim the finished length of the handles down to 57" instead of 52".

LAYOUT & CUTTING

The only pattern pieces provided for this bag are the Bag End (sheet 3), Media Pocket Flap (sheet 5) and Main Bag Flap (sheet 5). The rest of the pieces are cut by measurements given in the instructions with a rotary cutter, ruler and mat.

MAIN BAG PREPARATION AND HANDLES

1 Cut four 16" squares from Fabric A. If the fabric has a particular design motif you'd like to see centered on the bag, cut the squares from the fabric accordingly. Also cut two 16" squares from Peltex.

2 Apply the fusible side of the Peltex to the wrong side of two of the 16" squares. Set the other two squares aside for the lining.

3 On the main bag piece (with Peltex attached) mark a vertical line 4" in from either side of bag. (figure 1)

4 Using the Bag End pattern piece, cut four bag ends from Fabric A and two from Peltex. Fuse the Peltex to the wrong side of two Bag End pieces; these are your exterior bag ends. Set the other two aside for lining.

   Note: The following instructions for the handles are for the 9" drop. For the 12" drop, refer to the modifications detailed in the sidebar below left.

5 For the handles, cut five strips 2¼" × the width of fabric from Fabric B. Trim the selvedges. Cut one of the strips into four equal pieces and add one to each of the remaining four strips right-sides together with a ¼" seam. Press seams open.

6 Cut eleven 2¼"-wide strips from interfacing and apply to the wrong side of each handle strip, overlapping by ¼" as necessary.

7 Follow the instructions in the Essential Techniques for making the handles (pages 16–17).

8 Trim handles down to 52". Discard the leftovers.

9 Place handles on exterior bag pieces, centered on the 4" markings with the cut edge of the handle at the bottom edge of the bag. Be careful not to twist the handle. Pin in place, then mark 9" up from the bottom on either side of the handle on the bag itself. This is where the stitching will pivot and go across the handle before the top of the bag. (figure 2)

10 Begin at the lower edge of the outer bag, following the previous edgestitching on the handle. Pivot at the 9" mark, backstitch across the handle, then pivot and continue down the other side. Repeat for the three remaining handles. (figure 2)

11 To add the twist portion of the latch, choose the side you would like for the front of the bag, then measure down 4¾" from the top center of the bag. Center the prongs horizontally at this marking and mark prong placement on either side. Snip through all layers at markings and slip the prongs into the bag front. Slide the backing plate over the prongs and use needle-nose pliers to bend the prongs to secure. Iron a scrap of interfacing over the backing plate. (figure 3)

EXTERIOR MEDIA POCKET

1 For the media pocket, cut one 10½" square each from Fabric A and interfacing. Apply the interfacing to the wrong side of the square. Again, keep in mind the fabric's design motif, and how you'd like to place it, and cut accordingly. The pocket will be placed approximately 3" up from the bottom edge and centered.

2 Fold the pocket in half horizontally, right-sides together, and stitch along the sides and bottom with a ¼" seam allowance, leaving a 3" opening along the bottom edge for turning. Clip the corners diagonally and turn the pocket right-side out. Press, turning in opening edges by ¼". (figure 4)

3 Edgestitch the top folded edge of the pocket. Cut a 1" piece of hook and loop tape. Apply the loop side to the center of the pocket, with the top edge of the tape ¼" down from the top edge of the pocket. Stitch around all sides to hold the tape in place. (figure 5)

4 Mark a line down the center of the pocket, 5" in from either side edge. Mark a horizontal line 3" up from the bottom edge on main bag piece without latch. Place the pocket onto the main bag piece, centered from side-to-side on top of handles and along the 3" marked line. Pin in place and edge-stitch the sides and bottom edge. Stitch down the center marked line through the hook and loop tape to divide the pocket. (figure 6)

5 Cut two Media Pocket Flaps from Fabric C as well as two from interfacing. Apply the interfacing to the wrong side of each flap. Apply the remaining half of the hook and loop tape to one of the flap pieces, centered and 1" from top and bottom edges of flap. Sew around edges of tape. (figure 7)

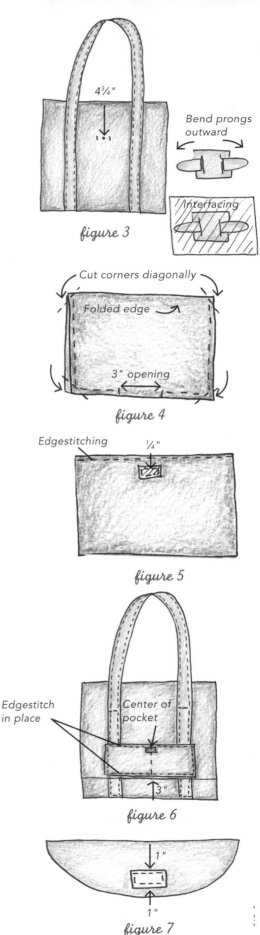

4¾"

Bend prongs outward

Interfacing

figure 3

Cut corners diagonally

Folded edge

3" opening

figure 4

Edgestitching   ¼"

figure 5

Edgestitch in place

Center of pocket

3"

figure 6

1"

1"

figure 7

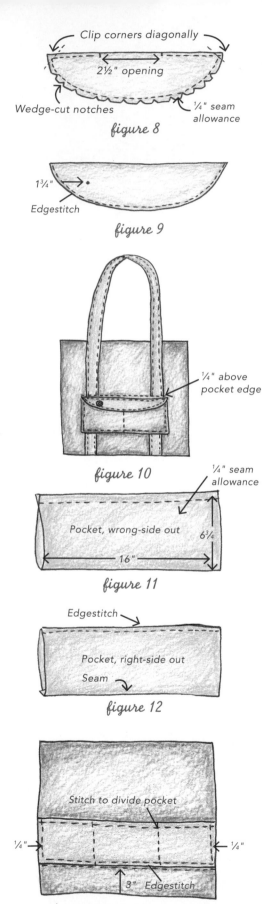

Clip corners diagonally

2½" opening

Wedge-cut notches

¼" seam allowance

figure 8

1¾"

Edgestitch

figure 9

¼" above pocket edge

figure 10

¼" seam allowance

Pocket, wrong-side out

6¾

16"

figure 11

Edgestitch

Pocket, right-side out

Seam

figure 12

Stitch to divide pocket

¼"   ¼"

3" Edgestitch

132

figure 13

6 Sew the flap right-sides together with a ¼" seam allowance, leaving a 2½" opening along the straight edge of the flap. Wedge-cut notches from the curve to ease the seam in turning and clip corners diagonally. Turn the flap right-side out, fully turning out the corners and curve. Turn in ¼" along the opening and press the flap. (figure 8)

7 Edgestitch the lower curved edge of the flap. Add the grommet for the earphone wire to the left side of the flap, centered and 1¾" from the side edge of the flap to the center of the grommet. (figure 9) Apply the grommet following the instructions in Essential Techniques (page 20).

8 Use a ruler to place a mark ¼" above the finished edge of the pocket. Align the flap with this line, centered above the pocket. Use the hook and loop tape on the pocket to help center the flap. Edgestitch the upper edge of the flap in place. (figure 10)

LINING AND INTERIOR POCKETS

1 For the smaller interior pockets, cut a rectangle 13½"×16" from Fabric B, with the direction of the fabric running parallel to the 13½" length. Cut one rectangle the same size from interfacing and apply to the wrong side of fabric.

2 Fold the pocket in half right-sides together so it measures 6¾"×16". Stitch with a ¼" seam allowance along the raw-edge of the 16" side to form a tube. (figure 11) Turn right-side out with seam along one long edge and press. Edgestitch along the folded edge. (figure 12)

3 Measure 5½" in from each end, and mark with a vertical line to divide the pocket into thirds.

4 Draw a horizontal line on the right side of both lining pieces 3" from the bottom edge. On one lining piece, place the shorter interior pocket along this marked line with sides of pocket and lining even. Stitch along the side edges with a ¼" seam then edgestitch along the bottom of the pocket. Stitch down each of the marked vertical line on pocket to divide it into three parts. (figure 13)

5 For the larger file pocket, cut a rectangle measuring 19½"×16" from Fabric B, with the direction of the fabric running parallel to the 19½" length. Cut one rectangle from interfacing the same size and apply to the wrong side of the fabric.

6 Fold the rectangle in half with right sides together so that it measures 9¾"×16". Stitch with a ¼" seam allowance along the 16" side to form a tube. Turn right-side out with seam along one side and press. Edgestitch along the folded edge.

7 Apply the longer pocket to the remaining 16" lining square, along the marked line 3" from the bottom with side edges of the pocket and lining even. Stitch along the sides with a ¼" seam then edgestitch along the bottom of the pocket. (figure 14)

8 Sew the lining pieces together along the bottom edges, right-sides together, with a ½" seam. Press seam allowance open. Cut two pieces of hook and loop tape the same length as the bottom seam (about 15"). On the right side of the lining, place the loop side of each tape length along each side of the seam, with the inside edges of the tape touching each other. Start and stop tape about ½" from raw edges of lining. Edgestitch tape in place along all edges. (figure 15)

9 To add hook and loop tape to the bag end lining pieces, fold the lining pieces in half lengthwise and mark the top and bottom edges for the center. Measure up 11" from the bottom edge and mark a vertical line, then mark a horizontal line ½" up from the bottom edge. Cut four pieces of hook and loop tape, 10½" long. Place the loop sides on either side of center on each bag end piece. Edgestitch in place. (figure 16)

ADD LINING AND SEW THE BAG TOGETHER

1 Sew the exterior main bag pieces right-sides together along the bottom edge with a ½" seam allowance. Trim the seam and press open. (figure 17)

2 Add the main lining piece to the main bag piece, wrong-sides together, with the small pocket section against the latch side of the bag and the large pocket section against the media pocket side. Align the bottom seams and use temporary adhesive spray to hold the layers together. Sew the layers together ¼" in from all edges. (figure 18)

3 Sew the bag end linings to the exterior bag end pieces ¼" from all sides.

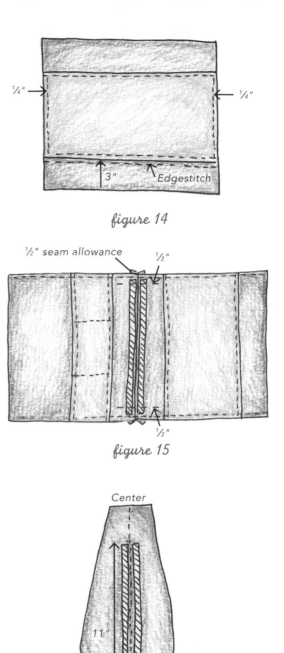

figure 14

figure 15

figure 16

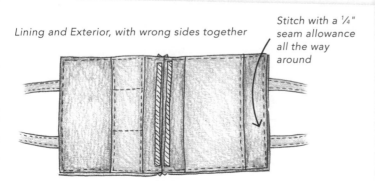

Lining and Exterior, with wrong sides together

Stitch with a ¼" seam allowance all the way around

figure 18

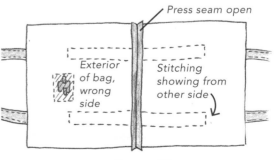

Press seam open

Exterior of bag, wrong side

Stitching showing from other side

figure 17

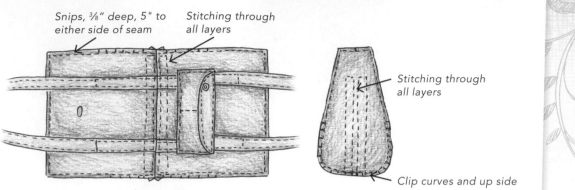

Snips, ⅜" deep, 5" to either side of seam

Stitching through all layers

Stitching through all layers

Clip curves and up side

figure 19

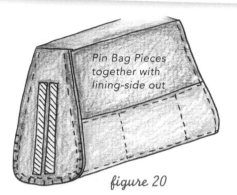

Pin Bag Pieces together with lining-side out

figure 20

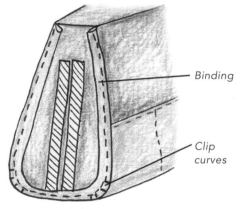

Binding

Clip curves

figure 21

Fold binding around seam

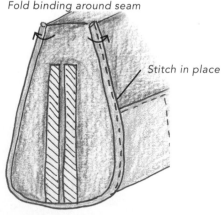

Stitch in place

134

figure 22

4 Change your upper thread to monofilament thread. To secure the hook and loop tape, stitch through all layers from the exterior side of all pieces (main bag and ends) about ½" from seams and the centers. This also helps to reinforce the bag to bear the weight of a laptop. (figure 19)

5 Complete a series of snips (no more than ⅜" deep) approximately 5" to either side of the bottom seam on the main bag and all along the bottom and curved edges of the bag ends. (figure 19)

6 Pin the main bag and bag ends together with the lining-sides facing *out* (right sides together). Start at the main bag's bottom seam, matching it with the center of the bag ends and working outward from there. The top edges of the bag should be even. Make additional snips as needed to ease the curves. (figure 20)

7 Stitch the bag together (with the main bag portion facing up) with a ½" seam allowance. Trim the seam to a scant ¼".

8 Cut bias strips from Fabric B, 2¼" wide. Refer to the Essential Techniques (pages 14–15) for more information on cutting bias strips. Piece enough strips right-sides together with a ¼" seam allowance to get approximately two 1-yard lengths. Press the seams open, then fold in half lengthwise with wrong sides together and press.

9 Cut the ends of the strips straight and pin to the interior seams of the bag on the bag end pieces. Clip the curves to reduce puckering and pleating in the seam. (figure 21)

10 With the main bag portion facing up, stitch following the previous seam stitching. Fold the binding over the seam and pin in place. Edgestitch the binding into place over the seam. (figure 22)

11 Briefly press the bag to soften the Peltex, then turn right-side out. Continue pressing, referring to Pressing Tips on page 22 in Essential Techniques.

BAG FLAP & BINDING

1 Using the Main Bag Flap pattern piece, cut two pieces from Fabric C for the bag flap, fussy cutting as needed. Cut one flap from Peltex. Iron the Peltex to the wrong side of one of the fabric pieces (the one that will face the outside of the bag). Apply the wrong side of the remaining flap piece to the other side of the Peltex with temporary adhesive spray. Stitch in ¼" from all edges.

2 Cut a series of bias strips from Fabric B, 3" × the width of the fabric. Follow the instructions in Essential Techniques (page 15) for making the strip. You'll need approximately 30" of binding for the flap.

3 Place the right side of the binding strip against the interior side of the flap, starting at one corner. Pin all the way around the curve and stop at the other corner, matching the raw edges of the strip to the raw edges of the flap. The straight edge of the flap will not have bias strip sewn to it. Stitch together with a ½" seam. (figure 23)

4 Open out the binding away from the flap and press. Fold the strip over the seam to the front side of the flap and press in place. Pin, then edgestitch the lower pressed edge as well as the outer finished edge. (figure 24)

5 Add the outer open portion of the twist latch to the flap at the lower center, with the lower outer edge of the latch 1" up from the finished edge of the flap. Cut a small horizontal hole, snipping until the latch fits nicely (figure 25), then put the latch in place following the manufacturer's instructions.

6 Add the flap to the main bag on the media pocket side of the bag; the interior side of the flap should face out (exterior side of the flap should face the exterior of the bag). The side edges of the flap will extend slightly beyond the main bag's side seams. This is to make sure that there is sufficient coverage when the bag is closed. Pin in place with raw edges even and stitch with a ⅜" seam allowance. (figure 26)

7 Cut a 3"-wide strip × width of fabric from Fabric B. Press ½" to the wrong side along one of the narrow ends, then fold strip in half lengthwise wrong sides together and press. Beginning with the pressed-under edge, place the binding strip along the top edge inside the bag, with raw edges even. Pin all the way around until the pressed-under edge is reached. Overlap by 1", then cut away any excess strip. Tuck the cut end inside the pressed-under end. Sew around the top of the bag with a ⅜" seam allowance. (figure 27)

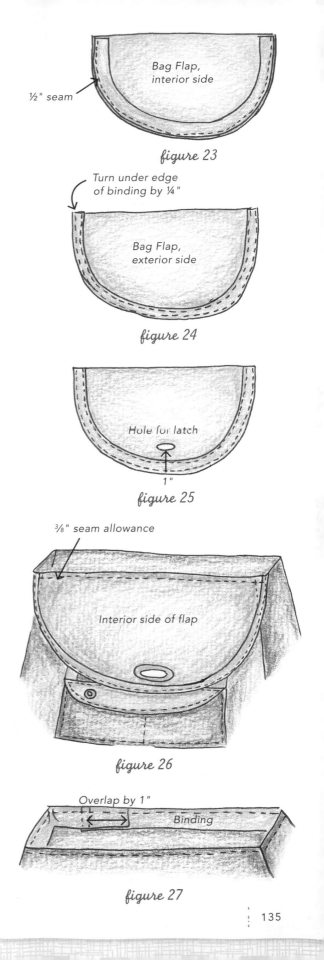

½" seam

Bag Flap, interior side

figure 23

Turn under edge of binding by ¼"

Bag Flap, exterior side

figure 24

Hole for latch

1"

figure 25

⅜" seam allowance

Interior side of flap

figure 26

Overlap by 1"

Binding

figure 27

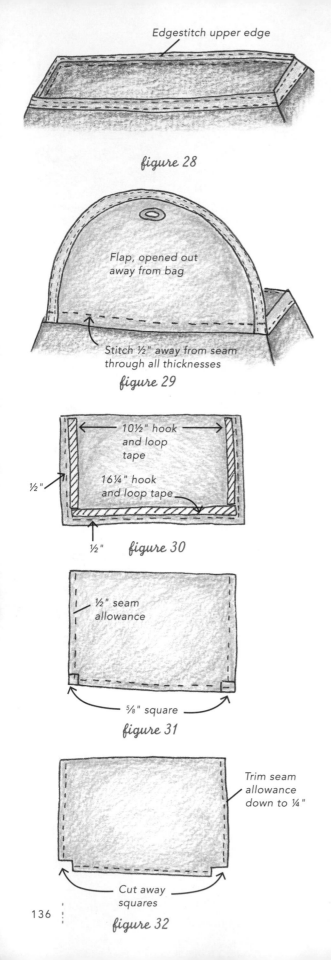

Edgestitch upper edge

figure 28

Flap, opened out away from bag

Stitch ½" away from seam through all thicknesses

figure 29

10½" hook and loop tape

16¼" hook and loop tape

½"

½"

figure 30

½" seam allowance

⅝" square

figure 31

Trim seam allowance down to ¼"

Cut away squares

figure 32

8 Open out the binding away from the bag and press. Fold the binding over the seam, press and pin in place. Edgestitch the lower pressed edge, then edgestitch again along the upper finished edge. (figure 28)

9 Open out the flap away from the bag and press. Slip the flap with the exterior side facing up onto the machine and stitch about ½" away from the seam through all thicknesses. This will hold the flap to the front side of the bag. (figure 29) Fold the flap over to the front and latch closed.

COMPUTER POUCH

1 To make the quilted computer pouch, cut two rectangles 17¼"×11½" each from Fabric A, Fabric B and Peltex, with the direction of fabric running parallel to the 11½" length. Fuse the Peltex to the wrong side of the Fabric A pieces.

2 On the Fabric A pieces, mark the ½" seam allowance on the sides and bottom. Cut four pieces from the hook side of hook and loop tape measuring 10½" long and two pieces measuring 16¼". Apply these pieces just inside the marked seam allowance. (figure 30).

3 Sew the tape in place along all edges, then pin the two rectangles right-sides together and stitch along the two sides and bottom with a ½" seam allowance. Mark a ⅝" square at each bottom corner, including the width of the seam allowance in the measurement. (figure 31) Cut away each square, then trim the seam allowances to ¼". (figure 32)

Up-Sizing the Computer Pouch

To make the pouch larger to accommodate a laptop with a 17" screen, make the following changes: Cut the rectangles at 17½"×11½" and cut a ¾" square out at the corners. The hook and loop tape strips will have to be slightly longer along the bottom edge at 16½" instead of 16¼". Cut the zipper panel strip to be 17½"×3½". Follow the rest of the instructions as written.

4 To stitch the pouch corners, open out the pouch and bring the bottom seam up to match the side seam. Stitch across with a ½" seam allowance. Trim down the seam allowances to ¼". (figure 33)

5 Briefly press the pouch to soften the Peltex, then turn right-side out and press the seams, being careful not to apply too much heat to the hook and loop tape.

6 Using the two rectangles from Fabric B, mark a 3" grid across the length and width of the fabric with a chalk pencil. The grid will not be even all the way across, but that's fine. The stitching serves to hold the layers together and since this forms the interior of the pouch, it won't show. Lay each marked rectangle right-side up and centered on one piece of the 12"×18" high loft polyester batting. Pin in place and stitch in ¼" from the edges, then stitch along the marked lines, both horizontally and vertically. (figure 34)

7 Trim away the excess batting to be even with the edge of the fabric. Place the rectangles right sides together and stitch, following Steps 3 and 4 to sew together, except with a ⅝" seam allowance. This takes into account the amount of bulk that the Peltex adds and makes the two fit together better.

8 Once the corners have been formed and seam allowances trimmed, place the quilted portion (still wrong-side out) inside of the Peltex portion. This should place them wrong-sides together. Work with the two pieces to align the side seams and layers. Pin along the top and stitch at ⅜" from the edge. Set this portion aside. (figure 35)

9 For the zipper panel, cut four strips measuring 17¼"×3" from Fabric C. Also cut four strips from interfacing and apply to the wrong side of the fabric.

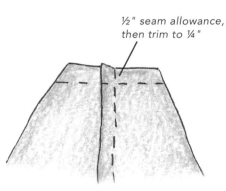

½" seam allowance, then trim to ¼"

figure 33

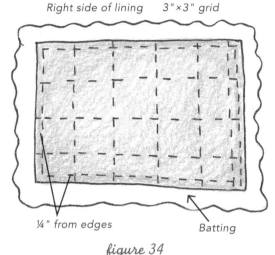

Right side of lining   3"×3" grid

¼" from edges   Batting

figure 34

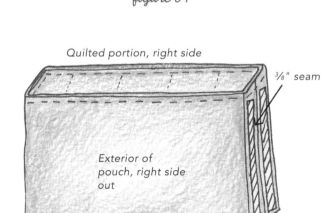

Quilted portion, right side

⅜" seam

Exterior of pouch, right side out

figure 35

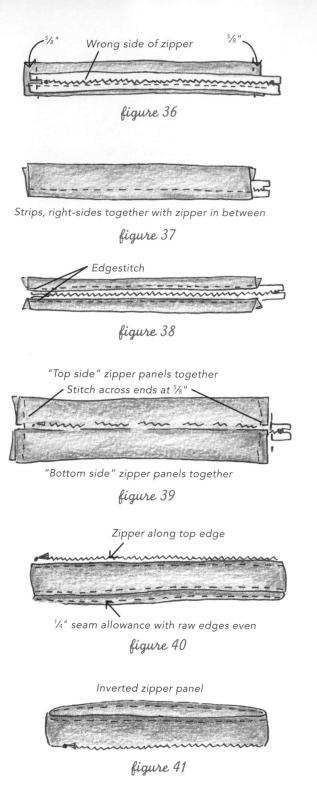

⅝"   Wrong side of zipper   ⅝"

figure 36

Strips, right-sides together with zipper in between

figure 37

Edgestitch

figure 38

"Top side" zipper panels together
Stitch across ends at ⅝"

"Bottom side" zipper panels together

figure 39

Zipper along top edge

¼" seam allowance with raw edges even

figure 40

Inverted zipper panel

figure 41

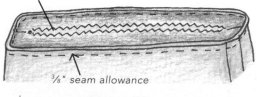

Zipper, opened

⅜" seam allowance

figure 42

10 Mark in ⅝" from each narrow end on the right side of each strip. Place the zipper right-sides together against one of the zipper panel strips; keep the top stop of the zipper just inside the ⅝" marking. Use a zipper foot to stitch down one side of the zipper. The zipper will extend beyond the length of the panel strip. (figure 36)

11 Place another zipper panel strip on top of the zipper, sandwiching it between the two panels, right-sides together and ends even. Follow the previous stitching and stitch in place. (figure 37) Repeat for the other side of the zipper with the two remaining panels.

12 Open out the zipper panels to each side of the zipper and press. Edgestitch next to the zipper on either side with right side of zipper facing up, starting and stopping within the ⅝" markings. (figure 38)

13 Place the two exterior zipper panel pieces with right sides together, aligning raw edges. Pin then sew the short ends with a ⅝" seam allowance. Place the two interior/lining pieces with right sides together and sew the same way. The stitched exterior panels will be on one side of the zipper and the interior/lining pieces on the opposite side of the zipper, as shown. (figure 39)

14 Stitch across the teeth of the excess zipper at the seam allowance several times and then cut away the excess zipper. Clip the ⅝" seams sewn in Step 13 at the junction of the two sides and trim the seam allowances to ¼".

15 Turn the zipper panels right-side out with the exterior zipper panel facing out. The interior/lining panel will nest inside the exterior panel, with the wrong side of the exterior panel facing the wrong side of the interior/lining panel. Align the bottom raw edges of the panels and stitch them together, ¼" in from edges. (figure 40)

16 Now unzip the zipper and invert the panel so that the stitched-together raw edges are at the top and the zipper is at the bottom. (figure 41) Place this inverted panel inside the computer pouch, aligning raw edges of panel with top raw edges of pouch, and matching side seams. Pin in place and sew with a ⅜" seam allowance. Keep the zipper unzipped for Steps 17–20. (figure 42)

17 Cut a 3"-wide strip × width of fabric from Fabric B. Press ½" to the wrong side along one of the narrow ends, then fold strip in half lengthwise wrong sides together and press.

18 Starting with the pressed-under end, pin along the inside top edge (the zipper pouch is still inverted). Overlap the binding by 1" and trim excess binding. Tuck the cut end inside the pressed-under end, and pin. Stitch around the top edge with a ⅜" seam allowance. (figure 43)

19 Open out the binding away from the pouch and press. Fold the strip over the seam to the exterior. Pin, then edgestitch the lower pressed edge in place, through all layers. (figure 44)

20 Pull up the zipper panel so the zipper is on top (the panel is above the pouch) and press. Pin in place and stitch along the top finished edge of the binding, through all layers, to hold the zipper panel in place. (figure 45)

21 Zip the zipper closed and add the zipper charm. Place the pouch inside the computer bag, carefully positioning the hook and loop tape so the pouch is centered inside the bag.

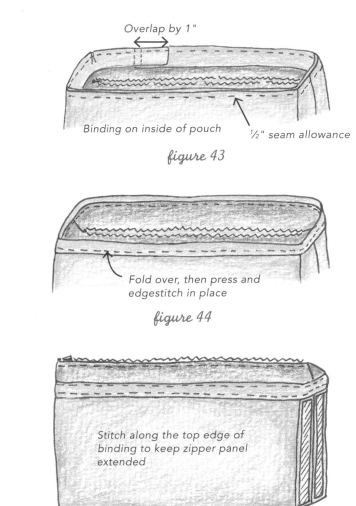

Overlap by 1"

Binding on inside of pouch   ½" seam allowance

figure 43

Fold over, then press and edgestitch in place

figure 44

Stitch along the top edge of binding to keep zipper panel extended

figure 45

RESOURCES

I receive a lot of questions about where to find the fabrics and hardware I use. Fabrics change seasonally, so you can't always find the exact fabrics, but I've listed some of my favorite manufacturers below. Hardware can be even trickier to find. I've listed several retailers that carry my favorite products, but check out your local fabric and craft shops, too!

fabric

WHOLESALE ONLY

Andover Fabrics
1384 Broadway, Suite 1500
New York, NY 10018
www.andover.com

Free Spirit/Westminster Fibers
3430 Toringdon Way, Suite 301
Charlotte, NC 28277
www.freespiritfabric.com
www.westminsterfabrics.com

Michael Miller Fabrics
118 West 22nd Street, 5th Floor
New York, NY 10011
www.michaelmillerfabrics.com

Moda Fabrics
13800 Hutton Drive
Dallas, TX 75234
www.unitednotions.com

Robert Kaufman Fabrics
129 West 132nd Street
Los Angeles, CA 90061
www.robertkaufman.com

Timeless Treasures Fabrics
483 Broadway
New York, NY 10013
www.ttfabrics.com

buttons

Blumenthal Lansing
1929 Main Street
Lansing, IA 52151
www.blumenthallansing.com

JHB International
1955 South Quince Street
Denver, CO 80231
www.buttons.com

bag hardware

The Buckle Guy
www.buckleguy.com
This is my favorite resource for snaps and latches. He has top-quality materials.

Atelier De Happa
http://atelierdehappa.com
Atelier De Happa carries the oh-so-perfect zipper charms from Inazuma, as well as other bag hardware.

Purl Soho
www.purlsoho.com

Hanah Silk
www.artemisinc.com

Purse Supply Depot
4060 North Palm Street, Suite 601
Fullerton, CA 92835
www.pursesupplydepot.com

Prym Consumer USA Inc.
P.O. Box 5028
Spartanburg, SC 29304
www.dritz.com

INDEX

www.fwmedia.com

15 14 13 12 11   5 4 3 2 1

DISTRIBUTED IN CANADA BY FRASER DIRECT
100 Armstrong Avenue
Georgetown, ON, Canada L7G 5S4
Tel: (905) 877-4411

DISTRIBUTED IN THE U.K. AND EUROPE BY
F&W MEDIA INTERNATIONAL
Brunel House, Newton Abbot, Devon, TQ12 4PU, England
Tel: (+44) 1626 323200, Fax: (+44) 1626 323319
E-mail: enquiries@fwmedia.com

DISTRIBUTED IN AUSTRALIA BY CAPRICORN LINK
P.O. Box 704, S. Windsor NSW, 2756 Australia
Tel: (02) 4577-3555

SRN: Z9866
ISBN-13: 978-1-4402-1415-8
ISBN-10: 1-4402-1415-8

EDITED BY Vanessa Lyman
COVER DESIGNED BY Michelle Thompson
INTERIOR DESIGNED BY Karla Baker
PRODUCTION COORDINATED BY Greg Nock
SEWN SAMPLES & ILLUSTRATIONS BY Kay Whitt
STYLING BY Jodi Kahn
PHOTOGRAPHY BY Scott Jones Photography, except for pages 11–23 by Christine Polomsky

about the author

"Love what you do, and you will never work a day in your life."

In a nutshell, this quote describes exactly the way Kay Whitt feels about her work as a pattern designer for clothing and accessories. After spending nine years as an elementary school teacher (sewing in her spare time), she resigned from teaching and launched her pattern company. Since then, Kay has earned a reputation for her innovative designs and clear instructions, making her patterns some of the most popular in the marketplace, and written the bestselling *Sew Serendipity*.

Kay resides in Texas with her husband, Keith, and their bird, ET. She is always busy working on something new and exciting and never tires of sharing her passion for design and sewing.

Metric Conversion Chart

To convert	to	multiply by
Inches	Centimeters	2.54
Centimeters	Inches	0.4
Feet	Centimeters	30.5
Centimeters	Feet	0.03
Yards	Meters	0.9
Meters	Yards	1.1

The designs in this book were created using Imperial measurements. If you plan to use metric measurements, the above conversion chart will help. Keep in mind that for best results, Imperial measurements should be used.

DEDICATION

This book is dedicated to my devoted customers. Your support of my work has made it possible to do what I love and share it with you for over ten years.

Thank you from the bottom of my heart!

acknowledgments

Whew! What a whirlwind this second book has been. Fortunately, I have the support of some great people who deserve much more than a simple thanks.

To my husband, Keith: thanks for seeing me through the writing of this second book. I couldn't have done it without your support and ideas! You are a great sounding board.

To my editor, Vanessa: thanks for everything you did to make *Sew Serendipity* such a great success and for carrying that enthusiasm right into this book. You always know what I want and work hard to get it "just right," even when that may seem a difficult task!

To Outlaw at Moda/United Notions: thanks again for so generously sharing your great fabric. Your friendship means a lot to me!

To Kathy at Michael Miller Fabrics: I love your creative eye and the fabric your company creates. Thanks for sharing many yards with me!

To my friends at Bernina USA: thanks so much for making the wonderful machines I use practically every day in my work. It means a lot to know that they are always ready to work when I am!

Needle?
Thread?
Fabric?

You're ready to go at **Store.MarthaPullen.com**! Find inspiration and instruction for all stitchers, whether you sew by machine or hand!

A Community of Crafters

Check out these other great sewing titles by F+W Media!

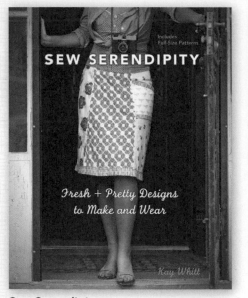

Sew Serendipity:
Fresh + Pretty Designs to Make and Wear
Check out Kay Whitt's first book for easy-to-make skirts, tunic dresses and jackets. A customized wardrobe is just a needle-and-thread away! Includes full-size pattern sheets.

Stitch by Stitch: Learning to Sew, One Project at a Time
You want to learn to sew? Deborah Moebes is your girl. In *Stitch-by-Stitch*, she gives you all the instructions you need to sew your way through 11 stylish projects. Includes PDF patterns on CD-rom.

The Bag-Making Bible: The Complete Guide to Sewing and Customizing Your Own Unique Bags
Lisa Lam provides the best bag-making technique instruction around, and lots of bags to go with it! Includes full-size patterns.